To Aunt Erma,
Love, Elaine Steeves
Sept. 2004

STEEVES AND COLPITTS PIONEERS OF THE UPPER PETITCODIAC

BRANCHES OF A FAMILY TREE

Previously Published
The Hoar Ancestry

In Preparation
The Hebridean Ancestry
The Newcomb Ancestry

STEEVES AND COLPITTS
PIONEERS OF THE UPPER PETITCODIAC

William S. Hoar

TANGLED ROOTS PRESS
VANCOUVER, CANADA
1988

Cover Illustration: The Steeves Homestead 1986
Sketch by Martha Henricksen Labadie

Canadian Cataloguing in Publication Data

Hoar, William S., 1913–
  Steeves and Colpitts pioneers of the
Upper Petitcodiac

  Bibliography: p.
  Includes index.
  ISBN 0-9692490-1-2

  1. Steeves family. 2. Colpitts family.
3. New Brunswick - Genealogy. I. Title.
CS90.S844 1988   929'.2'0971   C88-091372-X

Available from W.S.Hoar   *or*   Gerald G. Hoar
3561 West 27th Avenue   962 Salisbury Road
Vancouver, Canada. V6S 1P9   Moncton, N. B. E1E 3V4
(604) 734-8551   (506) 382-7759

Price $9.95
Postage/Handling $2.05

PREFACE

This is the story of my mother's ancestry from its beginnings in North America more than two centuries ago. Mother's ancestors first settled along the upper reaches of the Petitcodiac River and one of its main branches, the Coverdale or Little River. They came from Germany and England with the first waves of settlement following the bitter conflict that decided Britain and not France would shape the destiny of the land. They were God-fearing people who carved out prosperous farms from the wilderness and built comfortable homes, churches and schools; they raised large families, stood by during the American Revolution and watched, with some trepidation, the influx of United Empire Loyalists; they experienced the political upheavals that stemmed from the emergence of the United States of America, the formation of the Province of New Brunswick, and the evolution of the Dominion of Canada. After more than two centuries, their descendants are now widely scattered, a part of the fabric of both Canada and the United States. It is for these scattered families that I have tried to tell the story of the lives and times of some of their pioneering Canadian ancestors.

This book focuses on two pioneer families—the descendants of Heinrich and Rachel Stief who came with the Pennsylvania Dutch settlers of 1766 and the descendants of Robert Colpitts and Margaret Wade who were part of the Yorkshire immigration that took place in the last decades of the eighteenth century. More specifically, the account deals with the Frederick branch of the Steeves family and with the family of Thomas Colpitts and Ann Margaret Weldon, grandchildren of two prominent Yorkshire immigrants.

There are now many publications relating to these immigrant groups and the most significant of them will be cited in the pages that follow. Here, I acknowledge the assistance of many relatives and friends who shared memories of the places and times of my grandparents. It is not feasible to list all who have assisted but without special help from several, this story could not have been told. The substance of my Steeves family history came from three lovely ladies: Jane Wood who lives with the ghosts who roam the old homestead built by great-grandfather Ephraim, Alberta Dunn who grew up there in the days of our grandfather Stewart and Aunt Ethel (née Baird) who lived with all the many relatives while teaching in the local school more than three score and ten years ago. For three years, they have responded to my pleas with patience and interesting details. Likewise, much of the Colpitts family story has evolved from the research and records of Jean Colpitts Waddy who lives on the farmlands that Pioneer Robert Colpitts selected in 1783; she, through her contacts with Sterling Marsh, Elizabeth Goodwin, Anna Chavelle and the late Harold Colpitts, supplied much of the raw data for the story of the Colpitts pioneers of New Brunswick. I wish I had space to thank the others individually; I can only say to all my helpful cousins "Thank you very much."

Finally, I am most grateful to my illustrators: Martha Henricksen Labadie for the beautiful drawings of old homes (pp. 12, 52, 90, 116 and the cover sketch), the covered bridge (p. 106) and the sugar shack (p. 118); Diana McPhail who did the original maps (p. 8, 43, 98); and Carole Parlee who sketched the three plants (pp. 46, 78, 123) that were so prominent in the springtime diets of our pioneer ancestors.

W.S. Hoar
Vancouver
August 1988

CONTENTS

ILLUSTRATIONS

*I thought that, when I am beyond explaining,
they (my children) would want to know what
the world was like when my mother was young
and I was younger, and we two relics passed
together through strange times. I thought
I should try to tell them how it was to
be young in the time before jet planes,
superhighways, H-bombs, and the global
village of television.*

From GROWING UP by Russell Baker (1982)

EARLY ACADIAN SETTLEMENTS ON THE PETITCODIAC

During childhood, it never occurred to me that Acadian farmers first built the dykes that kept the muddy Petitcodiac waters from washing over my father's marshlands. Yet 200 years ago, small groups of settlers dotted the low hills bordering the marshes along the Petitcodiac River as far west as the present town of Salisbury (Map p. 2); there were larger concentrations of homes at Le Coude or The Bend (now Moncton), at Beausoleil (Boundary Creek) and at Village Victore (Salisbury). The marshes where I often picked goose tongue greens and swatted flies in the summer or tried to skate in the winter once produced lush crops of wheat, peas, oats, rye, barley or hay; the hillsides that I remember as a source of wild strawberries on hot summer days and of cold fingers and toes on toboggan slides in winter were probably the backyards of modest Acadian homes with their orchards and kitchen gardens producing turnips, cabbage and other edible produce; small flocks of sheep, scrawny cattle, a few hogs and poultry completed the farmyard scene. Near my home there were still traces of the old foundations of two Acadian homes when I was a child. A small chapel located near the present Bore Park in Moncton was the center of these communities and the Moncton area, for this reason, was often called La Chapelle as well as Le Coude.

My knowledge of the Acadians, like that of many others, was based on Longfellow's epic poem EVANGELINE. Yet the unhappy episodes at Grand Pré took place more than three years before the closing scenes of the Acadian drama on the upper Petitcodiac River. The story of the early settlements in Terre Rouge, as

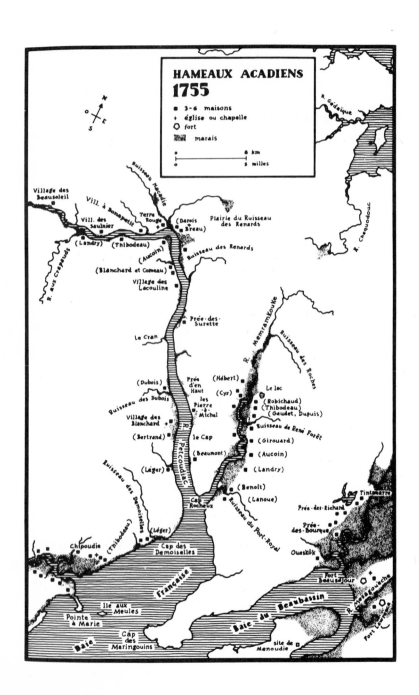

HAMEAUX ACADIENS
1755

- 3-6 maisons
+ église ou chapelle
○ fort
▨ marais

0 ————— 8 km
0 ————— 5 milles

R. Gédaïque

Village des Beausoleil

Ruisseau Macadie

Vill. à Bonapetit

Vill. des Saulnier

Terre Rouge

(Darois & Breau)

Plairie du Ruisseau des Renards

R. Chequodouc

(Landry)

(Thibodeau)

(Aucoin)

Ruisseau des Renards

(Blanchard et Comeau)

Village des Lacouline

R. aux Crapauds

Prée-des-Surette

Le Cran

R. Memramkouke

Ruisseau des Roches

(Dubois)

Prée d'en Haut

(Hébert)

(Cyr)

Le lac

(Robichaud)

(Thibodeau)

(Gaudet, Dupuis)

Ruisseau des Dubois

les Pierre -à- Michel

Village des Blanchard

R. Peticoudiac

le Cap

Ruisseau de René Forêt

(Bertrand)

(Girouard)

(beaumont)

(Aucoin)

(Léger)

(Landry)

Ruisseau des Demoiselles

(Benoît)

Tintamarre

Cap Rocheux

(Lanoue)

Prée-des-Richard

Ruisseau du Port-Royal

Prée-des-Bourque

(Thibodeau)

(Léger)

Chipoudie

Cap des Demoiselles

Oueskök

Fort Beauséjour

R. Aoussagouèche

Française

Île aux Meules

Pointe à Marie

Baie du Beaubassin

Fort Laurence

Baie

Cap des Maringouins

site de Menoudie

this valley was called, is largely a forgotten fragment of New Brunswick history—unknown to most of us who spent our early days there.

FIRST ACADIAN SETTLEMENTS

The land that became known as ACADIA included what is now South-Eastern Quebec, Eastern Maine, New Brunswick, Nova Scotia and Prince Edward Island. For unrecorded centuries, these lands were the undisputed domain of the Micmac and Maliseet (Malecite) Indians—highly resourceful and intelligent natives who travelled the waterways in their birchbark canoes, hunted the virgin forests and assembled on the peaceful coasts in the summer to harvest the abundant shellfish, salmon, eels and many other kinds of fish.[1]

In 1497, the Genoese navigator John Cabot, with the blessing of King Henry VII of England and the financial backing of the merchants of Bristol, landed on the shores of Eastern Canada. Between that historic date and the end of the next century all of the great seafaring nations of Western Europe probed ever more frequently westward to discover and harvest fish for the growing populations of the old world. By 1600, the North Atlantic seaboard of America was firmly incorporated into the European economy as an essential source of food fish and a rich reservoir of beautiful and much coveted furs. France, Portugal, Spain, England and Holland launched their fishing boats into the North Atlantic but when it came to land claims and colonization, the fate of this vast continent was decided in the long drawn out rivalry between England and France.

Location of homes on the upper Petitcodiac in 1755. Each solid symbol indicates 3-6 homes. Reproduced from "Le Grand Petcoudiac." Volume III of "Histoire des Trois-Rivières" by Paul Surette (1985). Maps by the author; graphics by Bernard LeBlanc. Courtesy Paul Surette.

Initially, the idea of colonizing the country and living in it permanently appealed to very few—least of all to the French. The first settlements were little more than coastal summer camps, bases for the landing, salting and drying of codfish. The fishermen went home to their families at the end of the season, to come again and make another start the next year. However, by the early 1600s King Henry IV of France was being warned that unless some permanent settlements guaranteed French claims, the North American lands would fall under the control of the English or the Dutch and the highly prized harvests of fish and furs would be lost as well as the coastal fishing stations. The French King reacted with a policy of granting exclusive fishing and trading rights to adventurous merchants who, in exchange for the monopoly, would transport and settle a certain number of colonists each year.

The project got off to a slow start but in 1604 a viable company was formed with Pierre du Guast, Sieur de Monts as chief shareholder, and in April of that year, the *Jonas* sailed west with de Monts in command of the party, Samuel de Champlain on board as cartographer and, among others, a distinguished Frenchman Jean de Biencourt, Sieur de Poutrincourt, a good friend of Henry IV and destined to play a major role in the early settlement of Acadia. These explorers touched at Port Royal which appealed to Poutrincourt and St. Croix where de Monts elected to spend the winter. It was a winter of extreme hardship and in the spring of 1605, de Monts returned to France leaving Poutrincourt in charge of a group of men at Port Royal, which was clearly the better site. Poutrincourt and his associates settled in and, unlike the seasonal settlers on the outer coast, planted crops and prepared to spend the winter in America. Poutrincourt had a keen interest in farming and dreamed of a colony of farmers in America; his men had time to attempt the first agricultural activities in Acadia. Although logistic support from the homeland was withdrawn in 1607, it had by that time been shown that Europeans could survive a Canadian winter and that productive crops could be harvested in Acadia; these French gentlemen (who formed themselves into the Order of Good Cheer) spent a pleasant winter in their Habitation at Port Royal (now faithfully reconstructed by Parks Canada) with plenty of wild game to eat and good relations with the Micmac men and maidens to provide comforts that they could not

4

bring from home. During the long winter evenings of 1606-07 while an easy sociability prevailed, Champlain was busy with his maps, Poutrincourt's fourteen-year-old son Biencourt was mastering the Micmac tongue and the scholar Marc Lescarbot was writing the verses and history of their adventure—now the basis of what we know of these early times. When all this came to an end in 1607, the English were establishing the colony of Virginia; this colony made a much more rapid start than the Acadian settlement, reaching a population of 3,000 within the first seven years.

How did Port Royal happen to be the locale of this first year-round settlement? It was perhaps fortuitous that de Monts landed there in the first place but Poutrincourt seems to have been on the lookout for good farming land since he had a cherished dream of a colony of farmers in America and a place for himself and his family; he liked what he saw at the gateway to the Annapolis valley. [2] Moreover, to Europeans of this century, the wealth of the Bay of Fundy was in the fur trade and not the fisheries. Unlike the cod fisheries of the North Atlantic which required European boats and men, the harvest of furs was dependent on the native people who trapped the animals, met the foreigners and exchanged furs for pots, pans, blankets and trinkets of all kinds. With Poutrincourt's interest and the time of his associates available, the great agricultural experiment started. In the long run, the productivity of the region was obvious and with the technique of building dykes and reclaiming the marshlands, the success of the Annapolis settlements was assured. When Isaac de Razilly brought the first French families to Acadia in 1635 an abortive attempt was made to establish a colony at La Have, about 45 miles west of Halifax ("as the crow flies") but soon the entire effort was concentrated at Port Royal. Within five years, de Razilly brought out 40 French families, the nucleus of all future Acadians. Marsh reclamation was already under way in the 1630s and by 1650 the colony was firmly established along the tidal marshes of the Annapolis River. This settlement and its subsequent expansions were based on not more than 250 original settlers (Brebner, 1927). By the end of the century, the population had expanded to 1,500 with an economy based on farming marshlands and utilizing the abundant resources of the woodlands and streams. These pioneering Acadians enjoyed good relations with the Micmacs and learned much from them, while charting a neutral course between the French and the English as these two great European powers struggled for the dominance of the North American continent. The highlights of this long struggle are given in the Chronology at the end of this chapter; our concern here is with the Acadian people who first settled the country where our ancestors later made their homes.

ORIGINS OF THE ACADIAN PEOPLE

For the better part of a century, the Acadians tried to remain neutral while awaiting the outcome of the French/English struggle. During this period their numbers increased at a very great rate reaching more than 10,000 in the 1750s. This phenomenal rate of increase, which saw a population growth from about 250 in 1635 to more than 13,000 at the time of the Expulsion in 1755, can be attributed to large families averaging nine children, excellent and abundant nutrition, the virtual absence of epidemics, and freedom from wars; while fighting raged around them, the Acadians for the most part, maintained their policy of "wait and see" and their young people were not decimated by the battles that killed so many of their contemporaries elsewhere.

Many of the first Acadians came from the La Rochelle area of France, a coastal region about 90 miles south of the mouth of the River Loire. Here the marshes were reclaimed by building dykes, and salt was produced by trapping sea water in ponds behind dykes where the water evaporated to leave the salt. The Acadians at Port Royal used their knowledge of dyke building to reclaim the tidal marshes for farmlands along the Annapolis River. With readily available timber, mud and sods, the mud flats were cut off from the flooding tides while wooden sluice gates *(aboiteaux)* swung open at low tide to permit the fresh water to flow out but closed with the flooding tides to keep back the sea.[3] While their pioneering countrymen along the St. Lawrence River were felling the virgin forests and pulling stumps to wrest their farms from the wilderness, the Acadians were raising dykes and building *aboiteaux* to create productive fields for their crops of grain, peas and hay. Some of these dykes as high as 2 m and 4 m wide with a road running along the top. Without added fertilizers or the necessity of crop rotation, the reclaimed fields gave high yields and could be periodically fertilized by admitting the spring tides to deposit another layer of mineral-rich silt.

Within forty years the population around the Annapolis River numbered 500; good marshlands in the region were gradually being occupied and young men were looking east where they had learned of vast meadows at the head of the bay. Acadians returning from distant hunts and the Micmacs told stories of great marshes around the Cumberland and Minas Basins; in 1672 a small group of young farmers led by Jacques Bourgeois settled at Beaubassin (head of Cumberland Basin, later the site of Fort Lawrence) and by 1680, the marshlands around Minas Basin (Grand Pré) were being occupied as well (Harris and Warkentin, 1974). These settlements expanded much more rapidly than the original colony near Port Royal.

Population pressure was not the only factor encouraging emigration from the Annapolis valley. The government at Port Royal, whether French or English, encouraged trade with the homelands and discouraged dealings with the aggressive New Englanders—their recognized enemies. At Beaubassin and elsewhere around the head of the Bay of Fundy, the settlers were sufficiently distant from the watchful eyes of government to promote the best possible commercial deals and, moreover, they were even better located for the fur trade. Here, they traded freely with New England vessels that came their way; they built their own ships and sailed to Boston and Louisbourg; they drove their cattle and sheep overland and hauled their grains to Baie Verte and Tatamagouche on Northumberland Strait, where the ships from Louisbourg picked up their produce in exchange for hard cash. Much of the cash eventually found its way to New England for the purchase of tools, mill parts, cloth, tobacco, pipes, molasses, brandy or other comforts that their land did not provide.

ACADIAN FARMERS ON THE PETITCODIAC

The adventures of Pierre Thibaudeau, the miller of Prèe-Ronde, were outlined in the first of this series of booklets. In 1698, he and his small party sailed west from Port Royal and discovered

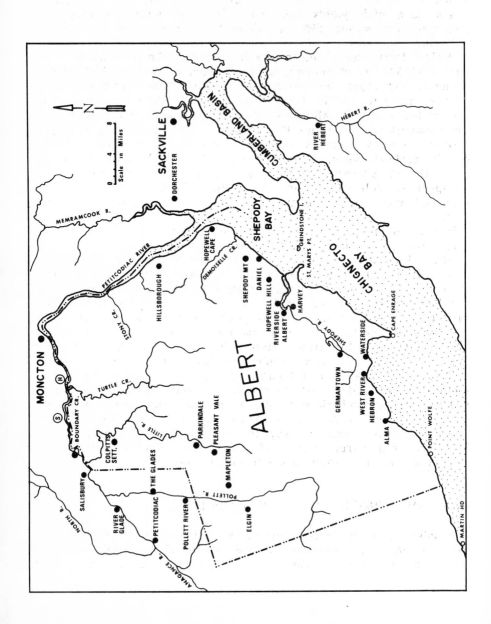

fine marshlands along the Shepody River in what later became south-eastern New Brunswick (Map p. 8). These hardy Acadians are thought to have been the first Europeans to explore Chignecto and Shepody Bays. Before them, only the native Indians coasted along the shores and threaded the three main rivers that drain into Shepody Bay (the Shepody, the Memramcook, and the Petitcodiac). In their birch bark canoes they could paddle up the Memramcook or the Petitcodiac Rivers and portage into streams draining into Shediac Bay to reach the east coast of New Brunswick; from the upper Petitcodiac, which is formed by the confluence of the Anagance and North Rivers, they had access by short portages to the drainage basin of the St. John River and the lands beyond (Webster, 1940). In several places along the Petitcodiac, traces of these early portages or burial sites have been recognized (Pitcombe, 1969).

For six years, until his death on 18 December 1704, Pierre Thibaudeau toiled tirelessly to develop the Shepody Bay colony and to secure title to its marshlands, the focus of his dreams. He saw several of his sons married and settled in snug homes while many former friends from Port Royal became their neighbors but his dream of a seigneury was never realized. In the end, these Acadians, like those on the south shore of the Bay of Fundy, were driven forever from their homes. Before this happened, however, there was a rapid colonization of the marshlands along the Shepody, Memramcook and Petitcodiac Rivers and the area became widely known throughout Acadia as Trois-Rivières.

On his first voyage across the bay, Pierre Thibaudeau was accompanied by his friend and neighbor Pierre Gaudet who subsequently pioneered the colonies on the Memramcook. Another neighbor, Guillaume Blanchard, who had a large boat, sailed with a party when Thibaudeau started off on his July expedition of 1698; Blanchard and his friends explored the Petitcodiac River where in 1698-99, they settled on a site near the present community of

---

Albert County, New Brunswick and the Petitcodiac River. Approximate location of Steeves and Hoar homesteads indicated by circled S and H.

Hillsborough. So it went, settlers returned to Port Royal with glowing accounts of the new marshlands and excited others to dream of tidy homes in a new region. By mid-century, when the settlements came to an end, the population of Trois-Rivières reached about 1,000 and most of the marshlands were occupied (Map p. 2); a string of hamlets stretched along the three rivers with major concentrations at several points on the Petitcodiac: Hillsborough (Blanchard), Stony Creek (Le Cren), the mouth of Turtle Creek (Le Village), Moncton (Le Coude), Boundary Creek (Beausoleil), and Salisbury (Village Victore).

ACADIAN SETTLERS WEST OF LE COUDE

The Steeves and Colpitts families first settled along the Petitcodiac River west of Moncton and this is the geographic area of particular interest in this book. The river and its estuary take their names from an Indian word that means "the river that bends round in a bow." The first recorded spelling of the word on a map of 1686 is Petcoucoyek but there are several subsequent variations of this (Ganong, 1895-1906). It is uncertain whether the bend referred to was the sharp one found where the North River joins the Anagance to form the Petitcodiac or the major bend that occurs at Moncton—the basis of the early French name for the location Le Coude and its English equivalent The Bend (Wright, 1945). For the past two centuries the Petitcodiac River valley has been a productive farming region where the land rises from near sea level, through marshlands and intervales to ridges that do not exceed 700 ft in height; locally these ridges are called "mountains."

The lives of the earliest settlers along the upper Petitcodiac River followed a pattern similar to life elsewhere throughout Acadia. Typically there were groups of three to six homes that formed small hamlets rather than villages. These groups were based on kinship or friendships, held together by common needs of maintaining an area of dyked marshlands, assisting with major tasks such as haymaking, hauling firewood, raising the frame for a new building, sharing a communal oven or merely for sociability. Their small tidy homes (often less than 800 sq ft in area) were of wood construction with stone foundations, thatched or grass roofs, and walls insulated with a mixture of clay and marsh grass (Daigle, 1984). One or two rooms formed the ground floor while sleeping quarters were above, beneath the steep roof. Life in the home centered around a large open fireplace used for cooking as well as warmth. There was an outdoor oven (sometimes an extension of the indoor fireplace) and here the hearty loaves of whole grain bread were baked in a daily ritual. Chairs, tables, shelves, cupboards and spinning wheels were made on the spot although metal parts, cooking pots, mill irons and such hardware had to be purchased—usually from the crafty New Englanders.

In the environs of the house, a well from which water was drawn by hand, an outhouse and a pile of firewood were essential elements of the homey picture. Kitchen gardens that produced an abundance of food, particularly cabbage and turnips used with some salt pork to make a rich soup, were fenced to protect them from the barnyard animals that ranged nearby. Sheep, hogs, horned cattle and poultry produced ample meat while venison or other game from the nearby forests added variety; leather, wool, and feathers were essential by-products. The land could also be counted on to produce small fruits and in most places apples were grown. The Petitcodiac was a rich source of fresh fish (salmon, smelt, gaspereaux, shad) while the local streams yielded speckled trout.

Life was timed by the tides that flushed the Petitcodiac estuary twice daily. The very long Bay of Fundy narrows like a funnel to create the estuary of the Petitcodiac where the water rushes northward in some of the world's highest tides. The "first of the tide" at the estuary's major bend (Moncton) is a tumbling wall of water that may reach a height of seven feet during the spring tides (average about 3.25 ft) and travels at a rate of 8-9 miles per hour. The BORE, as it is called, churns up the reddish silt and mud creating chocolate colored banks and mud flats that gave the Moncton area another of its early names Terre Rouge (red earth).[4] The tides fixed the times of day when the Acadians could come and go along the river, cross over to visit friends on the far shore, repair their dykes and aboiteaux or hope to capture fish. Tides also created slippery and treacherous muddy banks, much more difficult to live with than the sandy and graveled shores of non-tidal rivers.

The spiritual needs of the early settlers were satisfied by the

11

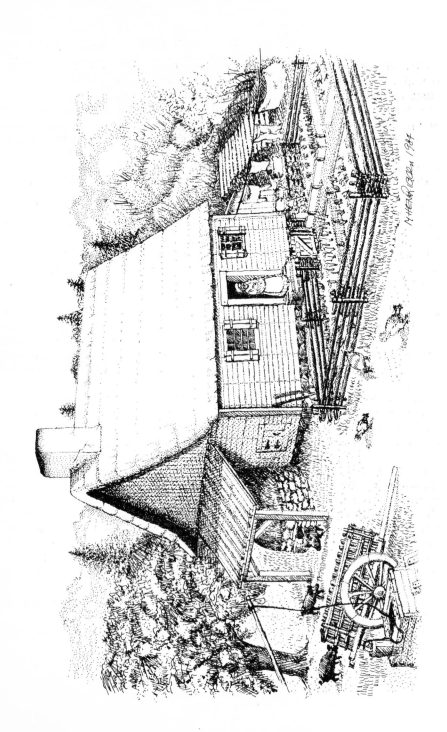

local priest who was also their main adviser and authority in decisions with respect to the English governors and their persistent demands concerning the hated oath of allegiance. The chapel at Le Coude seems to have been located near the present-day Bore Park. There were two other chapels in Terre Rouge, one at the present village of Hopewell Hill and the other at the town of Hillsborough.

THE WAR COMES TO THE PETITCODIAC RIVER

The settlements in Terre Rouge thrived for half a century and those along the upper Petitcodiac survived three uneasy years after the destruction of most of Acadia in 1755. This short respite was an anxious and unsettled time. Refugees with horror stories of The Expulsion and sad tales of the ensuing guerilla warfare were a part of everyday life. After Major Frye and his soldiers destroyed the settlements at Shepody and Hillsborough, the Acadians on the upper Petitcodiac must have realized that banishment was inevitable. Their options, however, were few: the refugee camps at Cocagne and Miramichi were sadly overcrowded and to flee to the forests was to ask for slow starvation; fatalistically, most of them stayed in their homes which offered food and comfort. Stories of guerilla fighting were many; Beausoleil, one of their number, was actively involved in the resistance. The Brossard family, originally from Port Royal, had settled on the upper Petitcodiac and Joseph or Brossard dit Beausoleil who commanded a privateer on the Bay of Fundy came and went to his kinsmen and friends at Stony Creek and Salisbury. Thus, news of the fighting and cruelties was not hard to come by. Today it is hard for us to believe the suffering and misery that was a matter of daily occurrence while the English tried to evict the remaining Acadians from their lands. One example will suffice. In the spring

---

Typical Acadian home. Sketch based on a painting by Azor Vienneau. Courtesy of the Nova Scotia Museum, Halifax. Painting titled "Acadian Home, Belleisle, Nova Scotia, circa 1720."

of 1756, George Scott, Commandant at Fort Cumberland (Beausé-jour), in the continuing guerilla warfare, offered a bounty for Acadian prisoners or their scalps "as they now act in conjunction with the Indians;" before this, the French had been buying British scalps (at the rate of 100 livres per scalp) for a decade or more. Thus we have the grisly picture of the French buying British scalps and the British buying both Indian and French scalps—a shameful and demoralizing situation (Bird, 1928; Webster, 1930a, 1933).

Several prominent characters played major roles in the final scenes of this eighteenth century drama. On the British side, Robert Monckton was in command at Fort Lawrence in 1752, became Lieutenant-Governor of Annapolis Royal in 1754, captured Fort Beauséjour in June 1755 and was active in the war until peace came in 1763. Lt.-Col. George Scott (later Maj. Geo. Scott) was also involved in the capture of Beauséjour and became Commander of the fort after Monckton moved on to become Lieutenant-Governor of Nova Scotia. Finally, Major Frye was in charge of the first expedition to evict the settlers from Terre Rouge. On the Acadian side, a colorful character Charles des Champs de Boishébert was established by the French on the St. John River in 1749 to protect French interests in Acadia and later to harass the English and protect the Acadian refugees. He and his rangers with their Indian allies carried on a spirited guerilla warfare for three years after The Expulsion, inflicting substantial losses on the British and helping many of their countrymen to escape and survive. Daily atrocities were committed on both sides (Bird, 1928; Webster, 1931). Lastly, there was the Acadian born Joseph Brossard dit Beausoleil, an enterprising man whose memory is treasured by Acadians to this day; his part in the resistance of 1755-60 was an active one (Webster, 1930a).

The drama on the Petitcodiac began to unwind on 27 August 1755 when Major Frye was dispatched from Beauséjour by ships with 200 men to go to Shepody "to Tak burn and destroy all the french in that part of the world" (Willard's diary as recorded by Webster, 1930b). A party of Frye's forces headed for Shepody where the homes were put to the torch, the Acadian cattle seized and a few prisoners taken; the majority of the settlers escaped into the woods. The remainder of the British sailed up the Petitcodiac as far as Hillsborough, destroying more than 300 homes and capturing 300 prisoners. Meantime, Boishébert, who had word of Frye's expedition, set out from his headquarters on the St. John River with a party of rangers and Indians. Arriving too late to assist the hapless Shepody settlers, he waited in ambush farther up the river and surprised Frye's men near Hillsborough on 31 August or 1 September (Pitcombe, 1969), inflicting such heavy losses that the English withdrew to Fort Cumberland. The entry in Willard's diary for 2 September 1755 reads "...Frye Come in with his party who had ben gon 7 Days from the Comp he Brought in about 30: women and children from Sherberdy and petitojack as they was Burning the mass house the Enemy Lay in ambush for our party Consisting of 50 men the party of french and Indians the number they Could not tell but itt was thought there was 200 hundred they fireed att our people upon a surprise and Killed Doc.ᵗ March and 23: men in the Engagement..." J.C. Webster refers to this engagement as THE BATTLE OF THE PET-ITCODIAC.

The second act of this drama was played out three years later in the spring of 1758. By this time the Seven years War and the English-French struggle for America were drawing to a close. On 28 July 1758, Louisbourg changed hands for the last time and by September of the following year Wolfe had captured Quebec. Throughout Acadia there was intense guerilla activity with Boishébert and his Indian allies harassing the British while Monckton and Scott attempted to remove the remnants of the Acadian population from the old lands where many of them, particularly in the Trois-Rivières area, had drifted back and settled again. Also important in the background for the final act was the meeting (2 October 1758) of the first legislative assembly in Halifax (the first Canadian representative body), and the development of a firm British policy to settle only Protestant people in the Acadian lands. The first call for new settlers was issued on 12 October of that year. Clearly there was no place for the Acadians in their original homeland.

The opening scenes took place on 28 March 1758 when a large party from Fort Cumberland arrived in Shepody to evict the remnants of that population. Houses were destroyed and women and children taken prisoners but no men were seen (Webster, 1930a). The last scenes opened on 28 June when some Acadians carried off nine bullocks belonging to a Mr. Allen who lived near the

Fort, thus igniting further retaliatory action by the British. An expedition was sent to Terre Rouge destroying homes of any Acadians who had returned to the lower Petitcodiac, reaching as far up the river as Stony Creek (Map p. 8). The expedition was considered a great success. The following quotation from a letter written at Fort Cumberland to a gentleman garrisoned at Annapolis (Ganong, 1930) reflects the flavor of the guerilla actions along the Petitcodiac: "...surrounded them, took nine prisoners, killed and scalped three, drove fourteen into the river, ten of whom were drowned...marched to the neighboring village, which they burned, with several barrels of wheat and pork; destroyed their gardens, brought off their household furniture, with forty sheep and lambs, and twenty-two pigs; killed three bullocks, with five horses, after which the party returned on board with their plunder." The date was 1 July 1758. Some writers have claimed that this expedition reached Le Coude (Moncton) but Ganong (1930) and Pincombe (1969) place the action at Stony Creek (however, see Larracey, 1985). In any case, the existence of upriver settlements became known, perhaps for the first time, and neither their remoteness nor the treacherous navigation of the Petitcodiac at The Bend could much longer protect them.

The final scenes of this play opened on 11 November, 1758 when Maj. George Scott with light infantry and rangers sailed from Saint John to put an end to all the settlements on the upper Petitcodiac. This expedition was timed to capture Beausoleil and his privateer since word had reached Fort Frederick (Saint John) that he was tied up for the winter near Salisbury; [5] moreover, from the standpoint of the British, it was a most favorable season to evict the Acadians, with a New Brunswick winter already upon them. Monckton's orders were specific: "...to bring them off [i.e. the Privateer and one of her Prizes] & any inhabitants he might take—and to burn and destroy all houses, barns, cattle grain & that he might find &..."

Scott's expedition anchored at Shepody on the evening of the eleventh and reached Point a Garde (Bore Park) at 11:00 pm Sunday 12 November. The tides and treacherous navigation prevented landing that day with the complete surprise planned for the inhabitants of Le Coude. Scott wrote: "The tide is the most rapid of any of the rivers in the Bay of Fundy, the Bore (or first of the Tide) running five or six feet high and sometimes seven in Spring Tides, which makes it extremely dangerous for Vessells grounding in the River, which we were obliged to do when we went up, and when the Bore came in it drove two of our Vessells foul of each other, did them much damage and I was greatly afraid would have wrecked them both" (Ganong, 1930).

Early on Monday morning, Scott dispatched a party of rangers and light infantry up river. West of Le Coude, the element of surprise was still with them and the settlers unaware of the destruction in store during the next 24 hours. The going must have been easy along well-worn Acadian trails and roads frozen firm by mid-November.

The privateer, which was laid up for winter at the mouth of Geldart Creek on the western boundary of Salisbury, was captured after a sharp skirmish and her prize easily taken at Island Creek which is located on lands later farmed by grandfather Steeves. Many Acadians escaped into the forests to spend a miserable winter and to surrender a year later, seeking shelter at Fort Cumberland; some prisoners were taken and transported to Fort Edward (near Windsor, Nova Scotia); none was deported (Pincombe, 1969) but their fates were just as tragic as those that Longfellow wrote about in EVANGELINE. Many Acadian homes seem to have been missed along the south shore of the Petitcodiac (Ganong, 1930) but when the rangers returned to the ships at Le Coude, only smouldering buildings remained along the upper Petitcodiac in the lands that later became familiar and deeply loved by our ancestors. This is now history and I leave it with a quotation from MacNutt (1962).: "...the point of view which emphasizes the rights of humanity unhappily bears little relationship to the facts of the Anglo-French conflict in America and is entirely out of context. The Seven Years War, like most wars, was a bloody business; and in the course of it both sides were guilty of worse atrocities than the expulsion of the Acadians."

The last entry in Scott's report of the Expedition to Remove the French from the Petitcodiac in 1758 reads:

Saturday the 18th

Weighed Anchor at 4 o'Clock in the morning from the mouth of the Petcondicke River and by 12 o'Clock at night arrived at this place [Saint John Harbor] with all the Vessells (Ganong, 1930).

17

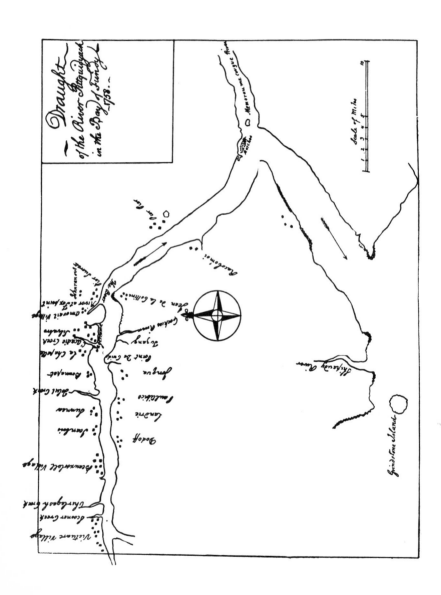

Draught
of the River Shignigsand
in the Bay of Fundy
1758.

Scale of Miles
1 2 3 4 5

As far as Scott was concerned this had been an entirely success-ful expedition. Le Coude with its smouldering ruins gave absolutely no promise of becoming a center of Acadian culture two centuries later with one of Canada's important French-Canadian Universities (see Schmidt, 1985). Nor could Scott have foreseen the upper Petitcodiac converted into a peaceful lake by the construction of a causeway in 1968, making it impossible for a privateer or any other vessel to reach Salisbury from the Bay of Fundy. The causeway neatly eliminated the navigational hazards that Scott encountered at The Bend together with much of the natural won-der of the tidal bore.

REFERENCES

Bird, W.R. 1928. A century at Chignecto. The key to old Acadia. Ryerson, Toronto. 245 p.

Brebner, J.B. 1927. New England's outpost. Acadia before the conquest of Canada. Burt Franklin, New York. 293 p.

Daigle, J. 1984. Daily life in Acadia. Horizon Canada 1(9): 193-199. *Also* 1985. 1(5): 97-103 *and* 1(12): 265-271.

Ganong, W.F. 1895-1906. Place nomenclature, cartography, his-toric sites, boundaries and settlement-origins of the province of New Brunswick. Trans. Roy. Soc. Canada Ser. 2: Vol. 12 (Sect. II): 3-157.

Ganong, W.F. (Ed.) 1930. The report and map of Major Scott's expedition to remove the French from the Petitcodiac in 1758. Coll. N.B. Hist. Soc. 13: 97-114.

From the report and map of Maj. George Scott's Expedition to remove the French from the Petitcodiac in 1758. L'Acadie Creek, now Hall's Creek; Isleel Creek, the area of the Steeves homestead; Beausoleil Village, Boundary Creek; Victuare Vil-lage, Salisbury. Coll. N.B. Hist. Soc. 13: 97-114, 1930.

Harris, R.C. and Warkentin, J. 1974. Canada before Confederation. Oxford U.P., New York. 338 p.

Larracey, E.W. 1985. Chocolate river. Lancelot, Hantsport, N.S. 254 p.

MacNutt, W.S. 1962. The making of the Maritime provinces 1713-1784. Can Hist. Assoc. Hist. Booklet No. 4:1-19.

Pincombe, C.A. 1969. The history of Monckton Township (ca. 1700-1875. Thesis Univ. New Brunswick. 339 p. [Microfilm No. 5694. NL-101 (1/66). Nat. Library of Canada.]

Schmidt, J. 1985. Les Acadiens. Equinox 4(2): 21-37. *Also* Reader's Digest (1985), June pp. 106-112.

Webster, J.C. 1930a. The forts of Chignecto. Author Pub., Shediac, N.B. 142 p.

Webster, J.C. 1930b. Journal of Abijah Willard of Lancaster, Mass. An officer in the expedition which captured Fort Beauséjour in 1755. Coll. N.B. Hist. Soc. 13: 47-75.

Webster, J.C. 1931. Charles des Champs de Boishébert. A Canadian soldier in Acadia. Author Pub., Shediac, N.B. 21 p.

Webster, J.C. 1933. The career of Abbé Le Loutre in Nova Scotia with a translation of his autobiography. Author Pub., Shediac, N.B. 50 p.

Webster, J.C. 1940. Historical guide to New Brunswick. N.B. Bureau Information and Tourist Travel. Fredericton. 119 p.

Wright, E.C. 1945. The Petitcodiac. Tribune Press, Sackville, N.B. 76 p.

A CHRONOLOGY OF OLD ACADIA

1497
First voyage of John Cabot who probably touched on the shores of Cape Breton Island. During the next century a few hardy European explorers coasted along the shores of Nova Scotia or sought refuge from Atlantic storms in her sheltered bays and inlets.

1605
Sieur de Monts established Port Royal in Acadia, the first settlement of Europeans north of the Spanish town of St. Augustine, Florida.

1607
Port Royal abandoned but not before successful farming demonstrated. English colony established in Virginia. At this time Shakespear's great tragedies were new in London theatres.

1610
Sieur de Poutrincourt re-established Port Royal.

1613
Virginia adventurers, under Samuel Argall, put the torch to Port Royal but the colony was rebuilt.

1621
King James I of England bestowed Acadia including Cape Breton Island on Sir William Alexander to found a New Scotland (Nova Scotia) to take its place with New England, New France, New Spain, and New Holland.

1632
France's claims to Acadia recognized (Treaty of St. Germain-en-Laye). Serious colonization started by the French. de Razilly brought out 40 families, the nucleus of the future Acadian population.

1636
Further immigration of 20 French families.

1654
Port Royal sacked and Beaubassin plundered by New Englanders who claimed the land for Britain.

1670
Port Royal returned to France.

1650-1700
Steady expansion of the Acadian population to about 1,500 settlers around the head of the Bay of Fundy. The last decade of the period was marked by French-Indian Wars on New Englanders and raids by the New Englanders on the Acadians.

21

1697
Treaty of Ryswick confirmed France's claims to Acadia but the ensuing peace was nominal and conflict between New France and New England continued.

1710
Port Royal captured by the English and renamed Annapolis Royal.

1713
Treaty of Utrecht. Acadia and Newfoundland ceded to Britain but the northern Acadian boundaries remained in dispute. Île Royal (Cape Breton) and Île St. Jean (Prince Edward Island) remained French.

1713-44
The long peace. Rapid expansion of the Acadian population to about 7,500.

1719
Construction of the Fortress of Louisbourg commenced.

1745
New Englanders captured Louisbourg.

1748
Louisbourg returned to France (Treaty of Aix-la-Chapelle).

1749
Founding of Halifax.

1750-51
France built Fort Beauséjour north of the Missiguash River and England built Fort Lawrence to the south.

1755
Beauséjour captured by the British and renamed Fort Cumberland. Expulsion of the Acadians. Battle of the Petitcodiac followed by five years of guerilla warfare. Acadian population over 13,000.

1758
Scott's expedition to the upper Petitcodiac. British capture Louisbourg and destroy the fortress in 1760.

1761
The Micmacs buried the hatchet and washed off the war paint.

1763
Treaty of Paris. All French possessions in America surrendered to Britain except the islands of St. Pierre and Miquelon (French) and Louisiana (Spain).

1764
Acadians granted the right to own land in Nova Scotia.

2

THE PENNSYLVANIA DUTCH

My pioneering ancestors were pre-Loyalists who settled in Nova Scotia prior to the formation of a separate New Brunswick colony. They belonged to three major immigrant groups: (1) the New Englanders who formed the largest of the pre-Loyalist settlements, bringing to old Acadia about 7,000 people between 1760 and 1768; (2) the Yorkshire settlers of 1772-75, in size a lesser wave (about 1,000 immigrants) but a particularly significant one in what later became South-Eastern New Brunswick and (3) the Pennsylvania Dutch settlers of 1766 who, in contrast to the waves of New Englanders and Yorkshire people, formed only a small rivulet but a rivulet destined to expand into a flood in succeeding generations.

Father's people belonged to the New England migration. Captain Eddy Newcomb of Columbia (formerly Lebanon) Connecticut arrived in Cornwallis (Annapolis valley) with his family in 1760; David Hoar of Brimfield, Massachusetts, with his progeny, landed at Onslow (head of Cobequid Bay) in 1761. In succeeding generations, our ancestors in both the Newcomb and Hoar families moved to Hopewell Township in Shepody; their stories are told elsewhere. Mother's ancestry is described in this book. This chapter and the next outline the early history of the Pennsylvania Dutch ancestors—particularly the adventures of Frederick Steeves and his family; chapters 4 and 5 deal with the Yorkshire settlers, especially the family of Robert Colpitts and Margaret Wade who came not from Yorkshire but from Durham County just north of the River Tees.

LAND SETTLEMENT AFTER 1755

With the founding of Halifax in 1749, Britain embarked on a firm course of creating a British colony in Nova Scotia. This was considered necessary and urgent to balance the French presence at Louisbourg and to secure the northern flank of the Eastern North American seaboard. For the next half century, matters related to the settlement of the colony of Nova Scotia consumed a very large part of the energies of the Governors and their Councils in Halifax as well as the Lords of Trade and Plantations who were responsible to His Majesty's government in London. This project drained more than £700,000 from the British Treasury during the two decades following the Expulsion of the Acadians.

The idea of ousting the Acadians was firmly linked to a policy of settling their lands with English-speaking Protestant people. The Acadian French were considered a serious threat as long as the outcome of the war between England and France remained uncertain; plans for settling their farmlands with English-speaking people were afoot even before the last of the Acadians had been driven from the lands of the upper Petitcodiac. On 8 August 1755, Governor Lawrence wrote to Colonel Monckton:

> When the French inhabitants are removed, you will give orders that no person presume to take possession of any of the lands until a plan for the whole has been laid before me, and terms of encouragement to English settlers deliberately found and made publick (Raymond, p.83, 1910).

At this time, the hope and expectation was that New England soldiers would opt to settle the Acadian lands when major military action ceased. But this did not happen—not because of lack of interest in the productive lands of the Acadians but because of uncertainties about the outcome of the struggle between England and France and continuing guerilla warfare with the remnants of the Acadian French and the Indians. By 1756 the Lords of Trade and Plantations were sufficiently concerned to write Lawrence:

> As the recall of the two thousand New England troops puts an end to any view which might have been entertained of

converting them into settlers upon the lands left vacant by the transportation of the French inhabitants, we shall remain extremely anxious till we hear what occurs to you with respect to the settlement of those lands, which appear to us to be an object of the utmost importance, and on the right determination of which the future strength and prosperity of the Colony depends (Raymond, pp. 83-84, 1910).

The officials in both London and Halifax argued that if more than 10,000 Acadians could prosper on the lands at the head of the Bay of Fundy an equal or greater number of British people should be able to live there happily. By 1758, the last of the Acadian settlers in this region, those living along the upper Petitcodiac, had been dispossessed and the remnants of the population scattered to the wilderness, especially to the northern part of old Acadia (now north-eastern New Brunswick).

Lawrence took action by issuing his First Proclamation on 12 October, 1758.[1] This Proclamation stated that "His Majesty's arms" had compelled the enemy "which formerly disturbed and harassed the Province of Nova-Scotia and much obstructed its progress, to retire and take refuge in Canada;" the Proclamation continued "a favourable opportunity now presents itself for the peopling and cultivating as well the lands vacated by the French as every other part of that valuable Province." The Proclamation was signed by Charles Lawrence for his Majesty's Council and circulated in New England with advice that proposals would be received by Mr. Thomas Hancock of Boston and Messrs Delancie & Watts of New York to be transmitted to the Governor or President of the Council in Halifax. The Proclamation was accompanied by a glowing, although somewhat exaggerated, description of the lands available:

. . . which consist of more than 100,000 acres of land, intervale and plow lands, producing wheat, rye, barley, oats, hemp, flax, etc. These have been cultivated for more than a hundred years past, and never fail of crops nor need manuring.

Also more than 100,000 acres of upland, cleared and stocked with English grass, planted with orchards, gardens, etc. These lands, with good husbandry, produce often two loads of hay per acre. The wild and unimproved lands adjoining abound with black birch, ash, oak, pine, fir, etc.

25

All these lands are so intermixed that every single farmer
may have a proportionable quantity of plow land, grass land
and woodland, and are all situated about the Bay of Fundi
upon rivers navigable for ships of burthen.

Many New Englanders were excited by these enticing prospects.
The time was ripe for an exodus from the old colonies. The population had expanded rapidly, good lands were becoming scarce
and the post-war economy in New England was very sluggish.
Moreover, British policy frowned on emigration to the west, at-
tempting to reserve the lands beyond the Appalacians for the
lucrative fur trade and to direct migration into the empty lands
of Georgia and Nova Scotia. Desirable as the Acadian lands were
known to be, the New Englanders were not inclined to move without guarantees of land rights, a promise of representative government, freedom of worship, and firm statements concerning their
obligations in the form of taxes and quitrents. Lawrence and
his agents in Boston and elsewhere soon realized that the conditions of settlement must be worked out in detail and the rights
of the settlers guaranteed.

A Second Proclamation (sometimes called the Charter of Nova
Scotia) was issued 11 January 1759. This stated that a number
of Townships, patterned after those of New England, each contain-
ing 100,000 acres (about twelve square miles) would be established
and that each would include the different types of most valuable
land, that the acreage allotted to each person and family member would be related to their abilities to plant, cultivate and
enclose the areas "subject to the payment of a quitrent of one
shilling sterling per annum for every fifty acres; such quitrent
to begin at the expiration of ten years from the date of each
grant. . ." This Proclamation further outlined obligations for planting, cultivating and improving the land and limited the area that
could be granted to any one individual in his own name to one
thousand acres until he could prove that he had fulfilled the conditions of the grant when he might make further applications.
The Proclamation continued with assurances of representative
government, courts of law similar to those in the New England
colonies and full liberty for all to worship according to their
consciences—Papists excepted (but see Harvey, 1933). No taxes
were to be levied or fees charged for granting the lands, and

assurances were given that His Majesty's troops would give protection and aid to the settlers. The Proclamation gave no guarantees of financial assistance but in fact Halifax did provide free transportation and small stocks of provisions where necessary to see the settlers through the first difficult years.

This Proclamation was circulated by agents in Boston and elsewhere and provision made for representatives of associations of interested individuals to visit Nova Scotia, to view the lands and select farms. The response was overwhelming. The first settlers arrived in 1760 and during the next five years an influx of wide-awake and industrious people imparted to Nova Scotia something of the character of old New England. Many of the settlers came with substantial personal effects and with farm animals; all came with the determination to create a free democratic society in their new homeland.

THE GREAT LAND SPECULATORS

Another significant aspect of land settlement in the latter half of the eighteenth century was the policy of granting large tracts of land to certain individuals or associations of individuals on condition that they bring and settle colonists on their lands. Many land speculators saw this as a golden opportunity to become rich through land sales, the collection of rents or exploitation of the resources of their lands. There were individual speculators; the most notorious seems to have been a Virginian by the name of Col. Alexander McNutt (Raymond, 1911; Brebner, 1937). There were also numerous government officials who were in a good position to know the location of potentially valuable lands; Lt.-Gov. Michael Francklin obtained vast acreages in the Chignecto region and subsequently promoted the Yorkshire settlement there. And there were such companies as those formed by John Hughes, Benjamin Franklin and William Smith of Philadelphia, who were largely responsible for the emigration of our Pennsylvania Dutch ancestors to the Townships of Monckton and Hillsborough. Between 1760 and 1773, while the population of the colony was no more than about 13,000, almost five million acres of the best land in Nova Scotia (which then included New Brunswick) were tied up by land speculators with very serious consequences to future development and orderly growth of the Townships. Absentee land-lords did not participate in the affairs of their settlers and many of the speculators did little to attract colonists, but held the land, hoping for an increase in its value. Eventually more than two and a half million acres of this land was escheated (confis-cated by the Crown) and sold at auction or granted to bona fide settlers. However, while the policy prevailed it interfered with the orderly development of community services such as road build-ing and dyke and sewer maintenance. The arrival of my mother's ancestors, both the Pennsylvania Dutch and the Yorkshire settlers, was related to the negotiations of the land speculators.

WHY PENNSYLVANIA? WHY DUTCH?

The short answer is that these people were German immigrants from Pennsylvania. They referred to themselves as "deutsch," which in their language meant German. There is, however, a much longer answer and to skip the longer answer is to miss a very exciting episode in the origin of mother's ancestors in America. The longer answer focusses on (a) the social, economic and religious background of eighteenth century Germany and (b) on William Penn's 'Holy Experiment' in the lands west of the Delaware River.

For most of the seventeenth and eighteenth centuries, devastat-ing wars raged throughout western Europe. The Thirty Years' War (1618-48) was followed by the War of the Grand Alliance (1688-97), the War of the Spanish Succession (1701-14) and the Seven Years' War (1757-63). By the end of this period, the Ger-man peasantry and the peasants in several other countries as well were destitute. Almost seventy percent of the population, together with their farm animals and much personal property, had been destroyed; bands of roving soldiers often pillaged the farms and were frequently billeted with the residents. In those days, the ordinary people had very limited title to the lands that they worked but paid continuously and heavily to their landlords, contributing both labor and produce. There was virtually no escape from this life of semi-slavery while, at the same time, religion that was often central to their lives was also subject to the ap-proval of the local authorities; Catholics were persecuted where

Protestants ruled the country and Protestants were persecuted when Catholics were in authority. Such sects as the Mennonites, Amish and other Plain People were particular targets of this persecution and were hounded from one area to another. A land that promised religious freedom and the right to participate in government seemed like the promise of Heaven on Earth.

Into the midst of this unhappy situation, a tall Englishman of stately mien came preaching a doctrine of peace and good will in 1671 and again in 1677. This man was the Quaker William Penn, a man educated as a lawyer and inspired by a faith that brought hope to many of the down-trodden of his day. His mother was Low Dutch and it is likely that he spoke and wrote the German language. The message that he brought was similar to that of Mennon Simon, father of the Mennonites, and the people he inspired were dedicated German farmers who already believed what he considered "near the truth." When, a few years later, these receptive people heard that this same man had received a vast tract of wilderness in North America where land could be possessed for the asking and where freedom of thought prevailed, their fondest dreams seemed within the possibility of realization.

William Penn was often at odds with the authorities because of his religious views and twice was thrown into jail for his beliefs. He was, however, a skillful lawyer from an aristocratic family who wrote forcefully and argued his case so successfully that he was not only released to continue his battles but elicited the support of Charles II, the reighning monarch. In fact, his family was well known to Charles since Penn's father, Admiral Sir William Penn, had made a substantial loan to Charles Stuart, the father of Charles II. On 4 March 1681, Charles II paid his father's debt of £16,000 by granting William Penn the Quaker a vast area of wilderness in North America. Penn's woods (Pennsylvania) thus became the tenth of the Thirteen Colonies and William Penn set about establishing its capital Philadelphia, the city of love, and settling its lands.

To this end he required colonists and many of them. Some of his English Friends, the Quakers, responded and formed the nucleus of the new colony but British immigrants tended to settle in the older, more established colonies—New York, New Jersey, Maryland and elsewhere. Penn turned to the down-trodden of continental Europe; he remembered the conscientious, sturdy, patient, hardworking and thrifty peasants of the Rhinelands and advertised the opportunities of his new colony widely among them. Agents were also dispatched to tell about the new country. The reponse was prompt and massive. Within a century of receiving the charter from Charles II, Penn's Woods attained a population of over 300,000 and as many as a third of these had come from Germany; about 75 per cent of the German settlers sought farm- lands some distance from Philadelphia and often remained as tightly knit communities, living to themselves, following a strict code of ethics and becoming known throughout the land as highly successful, dedicated farmers who raised a diversity of crops and employed the most advanced techniques of agriculture. Many of these communities still survive (Britt, 1973; Irwin and Lee, 1984).

There are many accounts of the hardships of these German migrants (Rosenberger, 1923; Dunaway, 1935; Wood, 1932; Diffen- derffer, 1977). The first group, arriving in 1683, were probably able to pay for their passage and purchase land but many who came later were penniless; they made their way down the Rhine with their families and limited possessions to the ports of Rotter- dam and Amsterdam, whence they sailed to Philadelphia and occa- sionally other ports of entry to America; long delays to load cargo in England were common. The ships were usually crowded, the sanitation disgusting, food and drink revolting and the length of the voyage unpredictable. Many who came after 1730 were referred to as Redemptioners, unable to pay for their passage and forced to bond themselves for several years of labor (usually three to five) before they could pay for their passage and be free to obtain citizenship and acquire land of their own. In short, they were indentured servants like many others who emigrated from Britain and elsewhere in that century. The indenture system offered high profits to ship owners; their agents traversed the Rhine countries persuading the peasants, often by misrepresenta- tion, to embark for America. A register of the arriving immigrants was maintained in Philadelphia after 1727 but this is not complete and German people who can trace their origins and times of ar- rival in America are very fortunate. Such is not the case with our ancestors, the Steeves.

HEINRICH AND RACHEL STIEF

Out of the thousands of German immigrants, Heinrich and Rachel Stief and their seven sons stand firmly in history on 27 January 1766. Where they came from and how long they had been in America before Heinrich signed the document that was to bring him and his family to Nova Scotia is unknown. Historians and genealogists have searched long for this information; perhaps someone will eventually solve the mystery but at present one can only speculate.

Hutchinson (1987) has recently discussed three possible scenarios for the arrival of the Stief family in Philadelphia. There is suggestive evidence for each of the possibilities but no proof for any one of them. We know that Heinrich was born about 1730 (he died 1778-80 at age about 50 years); Jacob the eldest son was born in 1749 or 1750 and we assume that Heinrich and Rachel were married in 1748 or 1749. At this time, Protestants were being sorely persecuted in Germany and immigration to Pennsylvania was tempting although emigration to Pennsylvania did not account for all of the German people who left the homeland; some came also to Virginia and other colonies; a group of Lutherans landed in Halifax. R.H.Hutchinson (1987) speculates:

1. Perhaps Heinrich and Rachel set out soon after their marriage in 1748 or 1749 seeking a new life in a land of freedom. This would fit with a Nova Scotia census of 1767 that records all seven sons as American; the theory would also support a personal communication from W.B.Oulton of Christina Lake, British Columbia who wrote (29 May 1986): " . . . the following item in Pennsylvania church records of St. Michaelis & Zion . . . Johan Jacob Stief . . . son of Heinrich and Regina was born 14 November 1749 and was baptised the 16 of November 1749. Sponsors being Johann Jacob Behnen and wife Magretha."

2. But perhaps they emigrated some years after marriage hoping to escape the hardships of the Seven Years' War; a later migration would account for the legend that only the youngest son Matthias was born in America; in this scenario they were probably Redemptioners, and Heinrich would have labored for perhaps five years before seeking naturalization, which

has been established as 1763, when he would be free to locate on a farm of his own. Nova Scotia may have seemed very attractive since a post-war recession was being widely felt in the old colonies.

3. Finally, Hutchinson suggests that the Stief family might have emigrated from Germany after the Seven Years' War with funds to pay for their passage and buy land and seeds. There is a family legend that they arrived in Virginia, put in a crop, lost it and decided to relocate. This theory suggests an arrival in America in 1764 with only a brief stop in Philadelphia.

At this time, the early history of the Steeves pioneers remains a mystery. Unless some new facts emerge, these hypotheses or some combination of them must satisfy family curiosity.

GERMAN SETTLERS COME TO THE BEND

Col. Alexander McNutt, a Virginian of Scotch-Irish descent, was the most ambitious and the most notorious of the promoters of land settlement in Nova Scotia (Raymond, 1911). He has been variously described as persuasive, resourceful, and utterly unreliable; whatever historians may say about him, the Pennsylvania settlers in Monckton Township owe their memorable voyage from Philadelphia largely to the colonizing efforts of this enthusiastic adventurer. Most of McNutt's settlers were Irish from his native land (Ulster); they emigrated either directly to Nova Scotia or indirectly by way of New Hampshire. However, he also located land agents and potential settlers in several other places, Pennsylvania among them. At that time, Philadelphia was a very logical place to look for colonists. During the century since William Penn embarked on his 'Holy Experiment,' the 45,000 square miles of wilderness that formed Pennsylvania had been transformed into one of the most prosperous and successful of the Thirteen Colonies (Coxe, 1794); the busy port of Philadelphia had become the second largest English-speaking city in the world. New emigrants from Europe, Germans among them, continued to pour into the colony at a time when much of the good land had been occupied and when economic conditions were depressed with the post-war recession following the French-English conflict for North America. Philadelphia was, in fact, an important distributing center for population in America and McNutt's schemes fell on very receptive ears. Many prominent Philadelphians, among them its most famous citizen Benjamin Franklin, became excited about Nova Scotia land development; others involved were the merchant and ironmaster John Hughes, the ship owner and trader Capt. Isaac Caton, Dr. William Smith the founder of the University of Pennsylvania, several members of the well-connected Jacobs family and a number of prominent merchants. [2]

John Hughes, a Welshman, was the most active of the promoters who eventually brought our ancestors to the Petitcodiac. E.C. Wright in *The Petitcodiac* (1945) records some of the correspondence and the prolonged negotiations, extending over almost two years, that preceded their departure from Philadelphia. All negotiations were painfully slow before the advent of the telegraph and the telephone. To expedite matters, Hughes dispatched an agent Anthony Wayne to look at the Nova Scotia lands and negotiate agreements. After a 13 day trip, Wayne in the company of Alexander McNutt and two other Pennsylvania gentlemen reached Halifax on 29 March 1765. His frustrating experiences are revealed in letters to Hughes; by 7 October he was writing about the "Despicable & Unjust proceedings of McNutt." In spite of the best efforts of John Wayne and the other Pennsylvanians, the Philadelphia companies were able to secure lands in only two townships: Monckton Township extending from The Bend west to the head of tide (Salisbury) and Franckfort at the head of navigation on the St. John River. The story of their negotiations as recorded by Wright (1945) is a fascinating one, revealing intrigues of administrators in high places, favoritism among well-placed families and individuals, and the great difficulties of long-range government in the horse and buggy days.

In the end four Philadelphia-based companies were granted land (Wright, p. 38, 1945): CLARKSON & CO. (Matthew Clarkson, Gerardus Clarkson, Edward Duffield, John Naglee); FRANKLIN & CO. (John Coxe, Jr., Benjamin Franklin, John Hughes Anthony Wayne); CATON & CO. (Isaac Caton, James Caton, John Relse?); WILLIAM SMITH & CO. (Thomas Barton, John Bayley, William Craig, John Hall, Joseph Jacobs, Israel Jacobs, William Moore, Hugh Neil, Joseph Richardson, William Smith). The combined shares of these companies amounted to about 23,000 acres in each of the 100,000 acre Townships.

John Hughes, on behalf of Franklin & Company, was the most successful of the Philadelphia agents. On 27 January 1766, Hughes and Anthony Wayne signed a formal agreement with nine heads of families (Matthias Summer, Vallon Tin Miller, Charles Jones, Heinrich Stief, Andrew Criner, Michael Lutz, Jacob Cline, Matthias Lenz, Jacob Treitz). This document guaranteed their transport to Nova Scotia and titles to lands in the new townships when they fulfilled certain terms related to the establishment of homesteads; further, there seems to have been an understanding that the land agents would provide some provisions, seeds, implements and so forth to see them through the early period of settlement. Four of the signatories (Miller, Cline, Crine, Lentz) withdrew before mid-April when the others sailed from Philadelphia bound for The Bend. Four of the remaining families were German (Summer, Stief, Lutz, Treitz) and the other was Welsh; Charles Jones, the Welshman, was related to John Hughes' wife.

The names of three other German families are often linked with the four that sailed with Captain Hall: John Copple and George Wortman (secured by Clarkson & Co.) and Jacob Ricker (secured by William Smith & Co.). These families may have sailed with the others in Captain Hall's sloop but this is uncertain. There is no evidence that Caton & Co. sent any colonists to Monckton Township.

Capt. John Hall's vessel arrived at The Bend on 3 June, 1766 and dropped anchor at the mouth of Panacadie Creek (now Hall's Creek). Muriel Lutes Sikorski seems to have fixed the date—uncertain for so long—by locating a letter written by John Hall and dated 13 June 1766; an excerpt quoted in a Special Supplement of *The Times-Transcript* (28 May 1983) reads:

> Deare Sir: We landed safe at Petitcodiac the third day of June and our people was well pleased with the land, but mighty tired out with a long voyage . . .
> And am: Sir, your humble servant, John Hall.

There are very few details of this memorable voyage; the name of the ship, the day of embarkation, and the log of the voyage are unknown. As far as the story can be pieced together from scattered correspondence, the voyage included a stop at Digby

SETTLERS LANDING

In honour of the first permanent settlers of Monckton Township, the Steeves, Lutes, Trites, Somers, Ricker and Wortman families who came up the Petitcodiac from Pennsylvania and landed on the bank of this creek June 3, 1766, this memorial is erected by Heritage Moncton, in cooperation with their descendants.

Erected 1983

or Annapolis where Anthony Wayne was landed, bound for business in Halifax; Wayne had been expected to look after matters related to the arrival of the settlers at The Bend but this was the last they ever saw of him. It is also known that the sloop landed the Rev. John Eagleson, a Presbyterian minister, at Fort Cumberland; Eagleson later became a missionary for The Society for the Propagation of the Gospel at Fort Cumberland. Beyond these sketchy facts, there is some evidence that Captain Hall proceeded 90 miles up the St. John River to land some cattle and to offer the colonists an opportunity to look at the lands in Franckfort Township.

It is apparent, from later events, that Captain Hall landed an outstanding party of colonists at the mouth of Panacadie Creek.[3] Their future must have seemed secure after signing a very formal agreement with their sponsors. Wright (1945) included the text of the agreement in *The Petitcodiac* with a photograph of a part of the last page showing the signatures of the eight German gentlemen (Charles Jones, the Welshman, made his mark). The gist of this document, extracted from its legal jargon, states that the company has secured two Nova Scotia Townships (Monckton and Franckfort), that the voyage to Nova Scotia will commence within the month of April next (1766), and that on arrival, the colonists could plant crops on any clear land for the first year. Further, that during the next summer (1767) a town would be laid out, where each of the signatories would be allocated an area forty feet in breadth and two hundred and fifty five feet or thereabouts in length (areas to be drawn by lot in a fair and candid manner) and that they would be given title to this plot as soon as they constructed on it a house with a stone or brick chimney and built a secure fence around it; possession of the lot was subject to a yearly quitrent paid to His Majesty and his successors. The agreement continued, stating that as soon as the Township could be surveyed and divided, each settler would receive 200 acres per five Protestant persons in the family, larger or smaller areas in accordance with family size; an unmarried adult son would be entitled to 100 acres and if married, 40 additional acres for his wife and each child born within four years from 1 May 1767 (Heinrich's two eldest might take advantage of this provision). Further, the agreement stated that after five years the settlers would receive title to their lands on payment to John Hughes and his heirs the sum of five pounds Pennsylvania currency per 100 acres of land, provided that the settler had built a good house with stone or brick chimney and fulfilled certain conditions of land improvement; these conditions included planting two acres of corn (grain), clearing, fencing and mowing one acre of meadow land, planting 50 apple trees and, after two years, cultivating a quarter acre of hemp each year; the settlers were also responsible for the surveyor's fees and would receive title to the land after payment of the stated sums plus any accrued interest. There were also general assurances for the group such that a "Water Lott . . . free and open for use of the persons within named and their Heirs forever for a publik Landing." This historic document, preserved in the Archives of the Pennsylvania Historical Society, seemed to provide for a secure future but as everyone who has looked into the history of these Pennsylvania Dutch families knows, it proved no more valuable than the paper on which it was written. In short, the settlers were abandoned by their sponsors in Philadelphia and received none of the logistic support required to make a comfortable start in the new land.

Wright (1945, 1961) tells what is known of the story of Heinrich Stief and his family during the next three years while they struggled to establish themselves in Monckton Township. Her sketch is based on oft-told family tales and two important letters that have survived the many years since our ancestors landed at The Bend. One of these letters was written by Parson Eagleson to a former associate in Philadelphia. This letter, penned 18 months after Eagleson arrived at Fort Cumberland, was basically a request that his colleague contact Dr. William Smith who headed one of the Philadelphia companies, and tell him that the settlers in Monckton Township had been supplied with basic necessities from Fort Cumberland through the action of one, Samuel Wethered, and that Wethered had gone to consderable trouble and expense and had every right to expect payment from Philadelphia. Details as to what was supplied and, indeed, whether the supplies ever reached The Bend are absent.

The second letter, written by Charles Baker the land surveyor in Monckton Township, is the more important document in detailing the hardships of the settlers during their first three years. The letter, dated 24 July 1769, was written to John Hughes almost exactly three years after the arrival of Captain Hall's sloop at

Panacadie Creek. This missive (reproduced in both   *The Petitco-diac* and *Samphire Greens*) states in no uncertain terms that the colonists that Hughes sent to Nova Scotia are outstanding settlers but that they are in dire straits because of lack of logistic support—particularly some basic provisions, clothing, working cattle (oxen) and other essential supplies. He went on to say that it is surprising that they had been able to survive under such desperate conditions, living as they do mostly on "Herbs which they Gathered in the Marsh in the Spring." Mr. Wethered's claims were also pressed once more and Baker stated flatly that unless support was forthcoming soon these excellent colonists would move elsewhere and Hughes would lose his entire investment in these valuable lands.

John Hughes probably never saw this letter. By the time it was written, Hughes was having problems of his own; as a Collector of Stamp Duties he had enraged Philadelphians to the point where he was forced to flee the city and the province; he died in 1772 and seems to have done nothing to assist the settlers for whom he worked so diligently before sending them on their fateful voyage in 1766.

The Hillsborough census of 1770 lists Heinrich Stief, Michael Lutz and Jacob Ricker who had married the widow of Matthias Somers—together with their families (in all 25 souls). Sometime between Charles Baker's letter written in the summer of 1769 and late in the year 1770, these German settlers had moved down river to make another start—this time in Hillsborough Township where matters were being handled in a much more business-like manner. The story of their difficult years in Monckton Township is interestingly told with all the details available in Esther Clark Wright's *The Petitcodiac* (1945)   and *Samphire Greens* (1961). My brief synopsis has been extracted from her carefully researched books.

THE FREDERICK BRANCH OF THE STEEVES FAMILY

My mother belonged to the Frederick branch of the Steeves family. Frederick, the fourth of Heinrich and Rachel's seven sons was about eleven years old when the family landed on the shores of Panacadie Creek. He had three older, 'teen-age brothers, Jacob

(then about 16) John and Christian; the three younger children were Henry, Lewis, and Matthias who was about five.
There are no recorded facts about Frederick's childhood, adolescence and young manhood. The first secure record is that of his marriage to Rachel Somers on 15 June 1780. He was then about 24 years old and she was sixteen. They settled in Monckton Township on lands that the family had vacated a decade earlier when they all moved to Hillsborough. Any more detailed account of Frederick's early life must be fiction based on the likely activities of a vigorous young male, growing to adolescence and manhood under the most rigorous of pioneering conditions, and the probable life of a young man who learned the tricks of succesful farming in Hillsborough; he courted a lass of his own race (probably making love in his own tongue), and then established a prosperous farm in the Boundary Creek area of Monckton Township, raised a dozen children and left descendants who have remained on his lands for more than two centuries. The records of Frederick's large and successful progeny argue for a healthy childhood, a vigorous youth, an active manhood and a concerned older citizen.

Alert, eleven-year-old boys are not greatly different the world over. Frederick would have been an active part of the confusion of landing on the shores of Panacadie Creek. It is not known how Heinrich and Rachel selected their first home site—whether by drawing lots or by negotiations. The location, eight miles west of The Bend in the area of Island Creek was a good one with extensive marshlands on both sides of the Petitcodiac. Island Creek, it will be recalled, was the spot where Major Scott captured Beausoleil's Prize in mid-November 1758. The map prepared during Scott's Expedition shows a number of Acadian homes in the region of Island Creek (Map p. 18) and it is not unlikely that Heinrich and his sons found some usable remains of Acadian activities; even after eight years of neglect there may have been a substantial base for a fresh start (perhaps a stone fireplace and chimney, the foundations of a home, a well for fresh water, some apple trees, remnants of fences and kitchen gardens, and a sturdy system of marshland dykes, drainage ditches and sluice gates).

All accounts agree that the settlers were deserted by their sponsors and that the promised supply ship never appeared. The older children, Frederick among them, would have spent busy days while the family lived largely "off the land." A healthy lad of eleven could have carried water, collected firewood, picked wild berries, gathered edible plants or assisted his brothers snaring rabbits and hunting. There were no schools in Frederick's childhood or even in his children's days; rural schools in this part of New Brunswick were more than a century in the future.

How long it may have taken Heinrich's family to discover marsh greens and acquire a taste for them is unknown; hunger is a very strong stimulant to the development of new tastes. Several species of edible plants grow on the salt marshes at the head of the Bay of Fundy (Szczawinski and Hardy, 1962; MacLeod and Mac-Donald, 1977) but only the goose tongue (*Plantago maritima*) and the samphire (*Salicornia sp.*) were eaten in my mother's home. These regularly appeared on the dinner table during the seasons when stored root crops were becoming dried out with long sprouts, and the sauerkraut barrel and pickle bean crock were empty. Marsh greens were always welcome while the family awaited the summer abundance of fresh garden vegetables. The goose tongue was more often served in my home—boiled with salt pork or ham; the fleshy samphire stripped from their woody stems was used in the same way boiled as a potherb but often also as a relish or pickle in spiced and sweetened vinegar.

There is a long-standing family story that the Pennsylvania settlers learned many survival tricks (including the use of marsh greens) from a friendly Acadian, Pierre Belliveau. There is no proof that Belliveau introduced them to marsh greens but the Acadians still use them and probably have since the days when their ancestors came from the salty marshland areas of coastal France; these plants are widely distributed throughout the northern hemisphere.[4] It is unlikely that the Pennsylvania Germans, coming from continental Europe, would have recognized marsh greens but the Welsh family of Jones might have known the samphire.

> *Come on, sir; here's the place . . .*
> *. . . half way down*
> *Hangs one that gathers samphire,*
> *dreadful trade!*
>   *King Lear. Act IV, Sc. 6*

During the three lean years in Monckton Township, the routine of the Stief farmstead was broken by several special activities. E.C.Wright in *Samphire Greens* pulls together the threads of evidence concerning fruitful contacts with the Acadians, the visits of Robert Cummings, prime mover in the settlement of Hillsborough Township, with his invitations to move down river, promising adequate support to make an easier start, of at least one journey to Fort Cumberland for supplies when the situation on the Petitcodiac became desperate. There are also oft-told tales of the Stief men building a boat, thus making travel easier than it would have been over the old Acadian trails. In later years, many of the Steeves family became involved in ship building, shipping and trading. Their first boat is said to have been a "dug out" and those who know New Brunswick forests today may wonder where a log of sufficient size could have been found to make a "dug out." Before the mid-nineteenth century, however, giant white cedars were abundant and Heinrich and his sons would have no difficulty in felling a suitable tree near the Petitcodiac. " . . . in the halcyon days of the timber trade, a tree that would not square to a length of sixty feet was not worth taking . . . (Spicer, 1968)." In places, the New Brunswick white pine towered as high as 40 ft (12 meters) with trunks reaching a circumference of 6.5 ft or about 2 meters (Wynn, 1985).

Frederick was a 'teen-ager when the family moved to Hillsborough. Robert Cummings, who was mainly responsible for the move, provided the logistic support necessary for a quick start and, while Frederick grew to manhood, the fortunes of the Stief family steadily improved. The records show (Wright, 1961) that within five years, Heinrich's starting stock of two oxen and four cows had increased to 12 oxen and 14 cows and that in addition he possessed a bull, ten yearlings, eight heifers, four bull calves, two mares, a colt, 26 sheep, 16 lambs, 6 hogs and 24 pigs. Further, the returns for 1775 state that he had raised 150 bushels of wheat, 18 bushels of rye, 16 of barley, 50 of peas, 100 of oats, 150 of turnips, 160 of potatoes and 30 pounds of flax. Moreover, the eldest son Jacob was now established on a farm of his own with his wife (Katharine Lutz) and two sons. By 1775, the opening year of the American Revolution, Frederick was 20 and probably spent long days working on his father's farm and acquiring the skills of a successful pioneer farmer. Map No. 132

of early land grants in the Hillsborough area (Dep't Natur. Resources, Fredericton, N.B.) shows very large acreages of Hillsborough lands registered in the name of Stief (variously spelled Steef, Steves and Steeves).

The first decade in Hillsborough was marked by three major events that profoundly affected the future of the Stief family: (1) the American revolution, 1775-83, which severed forever any legal ties with Pennsylvania and the hope of restitution by absentee landlords; (2) successful legal action against the land agents who had managed affairs so badly in Monckton Township and (3) Heinrich's death sometime between 1778 and 1780 at an early age of 50, followed by a family decision that Christian the third son and Frederick the fourth would return to the lands on the upper Peitcodiac.

The Stief family was only peripherally involved in the events of the American Revolution. There is a long-standing family tale of an invasion of Jacob's farm by a raiding party of New Englanders with the loss of livestock but, in the long run, the Revolution merely opened the way for the expansion of the Stief family holdings and for the settlement of two of the sons on lands in the Moncton-Salisbury area.

The Pennsylvania settlers in Monckton Township were not the only colonists to experience problems with absentee landlords. Wright(1945) details some of the difficulties in Hopewell Township, frustrations which led one of the settlers Thomas Calhoun to bring suit in the Court of Common Pleas at Cumberland for breach of covenant in performing the articles of settlement, claiming a considerable sum of money. Action was commenced in 1771 and when Calhoun died, his widow saw the suit to a successful conclusion and collected payment. This action in Hopewell sparked the German settlers both in Monckton and Hillsborough to take action. This action was probably instigated by Charles Baker the land surveyor who had not received his promised payments from the Philadelphia gentlemen. The judgments were favorable and in 1778 seven Pennsylvania Dutch settlers as well as Charles Baker and the Welshman Charles Jones were awarded large grants on the north bank of the Petitcodiac River extending from Hall's Creek west to the present town of Salisbury(Wright, 1945, p.47). The approximate location of their lands is shown on the map on page 43. It is evident that all the Philadelphia settlers who

42

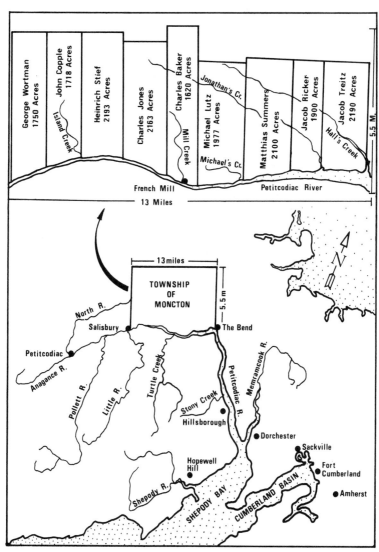

*Monckton Township as laid out by land surveyor Charles Baker;
data from Wright (1945). Plots not strictly to scale. Map
based on E.W.Larracey "The First Hundred p. 82, 1970. Courtesy of E.W.Larracey.*

arrived in 1766 finally received substantial satisfaction. In the case of Heinrich Stief, the judgment read:

> HEINRICH STIEF: £52 damages and £7 17s 3d Costs. Real Estate beginning at Stief's Point thence extending from the river to Island Creek joining to the Heirs of Charles Jones and then extending two thousand one hundred and sixty-three acres of marsh and upland.

These grants were all re-recorded in the Cumberland County Records of 11 November 1780. Later, when the Province of New Brunswick was established, the Governor issued a Proclamation (25 November 1784) requiring: "all persons . . . to exhibit and register all such grants of land as they may respectively hold under the government of Nova Scotia." In the end, only the lands of Mathias Summers were escheated but within a few years many new farms were formed from the original grants and as new settlers arrived in the Township the old boundaries were quickly blurred.

Heinrich's original grant (Land Grant No. 260) was divided into a western block of 1,159 acres which went to Christian while Frederick settled on the eastern portion (1,034 acres). Grant Reference Plan No. 119 (Dep't Natur. Resources, Fredericton, N.B.) shows that Christian and his sons also acquired large acreages both to the north of Heinrich's original grant and to the south of the Petitcodiac River in Coverdale. On Plan No. 119, the family name is recorded as STIEFF. In addition, Christian's original land holdings included parts of the Jacob Trites grant at The Bend; these lands were acquired through his marriage to Rosanna Trites (Cummings); further, Rosanna's daughter by Robert Cummings was awarded property in Hillsborough (Wright, 1961).

Within a century, much of Christian's property had changed hands through sales to incoming settlers. Frederick's descendants, on the contrary, continued to farm the original eastern portion of Heinrich's grant for almost two centuries. Maps of land holdings prepared in 1862 (Nat. Map Coll. Arch. Canada, Ottawa) show several different names associated with the original Christian lands while the Frederick farmlands are held by two of his sons Daniel and Ephraim; the family name was then spelled STEVES.[5] The story of Frederick's descendants, who have come and gone from these productive lands for more than two centuries is continued in the next chapter.

REFERENCES

Brebner, J.B. 1937. The neutral Yankees of Nova Scotia. A marginal colony during the revolutionary years. Columbia U.P., New York, 388 p.

Britt, K. 1973. Pennsylvania's old-time Dutch treat. Nat. Geogr. 143(4): 564-578. (April 1973).

Coxe, Tench 1794. A view of the United States of America. Reprints of Economic Classics. Augustus M. Kelly, New York. 1965.

Diffenderffer, F.R. 1979. The German immigration into Pennsylvania. Genealog. Pub. Co., Inc. Baltimore. 328 p.

Dunaway, W.F. 1935. A history of Pennsylvania. Vol. 1-2. Prentice-Hall, New York. 828 p.

Harvey, D.C. 1933. The struggle for the New England form of Township Government in Nova Scotia. Can. Hist. Assoc. Ann. Rept. (1933): 15-22.

Hutchinson, R.H. 1987. Those first Steeves: arrival and beliefs. Steeves Family Register 69: 19-21.

Irwin, J. and Lee, D. 1984. The Plain people of Pennsylvania. Nat. Geogr. 165(4): 492-519. (April 1984).

Larracey, E.W. 1970. The first hundred. Moncton Pub. Co., Moncton, N.B. 306 p.

MacLeod, H. and MacDonald, B. 1977. Edible wild plants of Nova Scotia. N.S. Museum, Halifax, N.S. 135 p.

Raymond, W.O. 1910. Nova Scotia under English rule; from the capture of Port Royal to the conquest of Canada, A.D. 1710-1760. Trans. Roy. Soc. Canada Vol. 4, Ser. 3, Sect. II: 55-84.

Raymond, W.O. 1911. Colonel Alexander McNutt and the Pre-Loyalist settlements of Nova Scotia. Trans. Roy. Soc. Canada Vol. 5, Ser. 3, Sect. II: 23-115.

Rosenberger, J.L. 1923. The Pennsylvania Germans. Univ. Chicago Press, Chicago. 173 p.

Spicer, S.T. 1968. Masters of sail. 2nd ed. Petheric Press, Halifax, N.S. 278 p.

Szczawinski, A.F. and Hardy, G.A. 1962. Guide to edible wild plants of British Columbia. B.C. Museum Handbook. No. 20. 90 p.

Wood, R. (ed.) 1942. The Pennsylvania Germans. Princeton U.P., Princeton, N.J. 299 p.

Wright, E.C. 1945. The Petitcodiac. Tribune Press, Sackville, N.B. 76 p.

Wright, E.C. 1961. Samphire greens. Author Pub., Wolfville, N.S. 94 p.

Wynn, G. 1985. Hail the pine. Horizon Canada 4(37): 872-877.

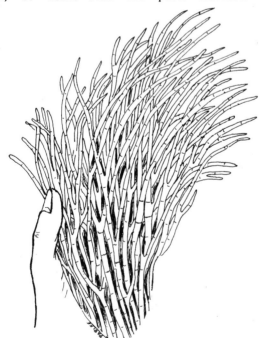

Bunch of
Samphire Greens[4]

3

THE STEEVES HOMESTEAD ON THE SALISBURY ROAD

When my mother was born in the old homestead (4 January 1881) Frederick's lands had already been intensively farmed for over a century. Mother was part of the third generation to be born and grow up there, to marry, leave and become a part of some other extended family. In all, four generations actively farmed these lands during a period of almost two centuries. The first half century was the era of Frederick and the second belonged to his son Ephraim—my mother's grandfather. Ephraim died in 1883. By the time my mother was born (1881), responsibilities had already passed to her father Stewart Alonzo, who made the important decisions for the next 25-30 years; finally, Stewart's eldest son John, my mother's brother, carried on the traditions of big farming for another half century.

FREDERICK'S HALF CENTURY

In the days of Frederick and his son Ephraim, the Steeves homestead was probably typical of Pennsylvania Dutch settlers in many places. Of these pioneers, Wood (p. 32-33, 1942) writes:

The Germans settled the land to remain there. . . . The Pennsylvania farmer showed a strong predilection for family-sized holdings and relatively intensive forms of agriculture. He looked upon his calling as a preferred way of life and not primarily as a commercial operation. He sought an acreage sufficient to feed and clothe himself well and to yield

47

the necessary means with which to secure farms for his children. In his work program, self-sufficiency was his ideal. Plantation agriculture and slavery in particular were anathema to him.

Self-sufficiency was a necessity in the days of Frederick and Rachel. When they settled on the farm in the early 1780s, the closest place of business was Fort Cumberland—a long trip on the Petitcodiac River with its treacherous tides and muddy banks. Legal problems were settled at Fort Cumberland and the purchases necessary for frontier life could be made only there. This was almost a cashless society. Services such as those of the blacksmith, minister, cobbler or doctor were usually paid by barter. A good farmer had an abundance of beef, pork, mutton and poultry; in season, salmon, shad and smelt were available for the taking from the Petitcodiac and most farm houses put down a barrel of salt shad for the winter. A variety of vegetables, small fruits and wild plants rounded out a healthy diet. The principal cereal crops were buckwheat and oats with some wheat and barley. Small grist mills were never far distant. The primeval forest supplied building material in abundance with small saw mills within easy reach. The extended family prepared for the long winter by drying, salting and preserving many of the foods so abundant in the long summer. The beef cattle provided leather for foot wear; the sheep provided wool to turn into knitted garments or cloth of several varieties from soft kinds used for women's wear and men's shirts to heavy horse blankets. There was plenty of work for everyone, no matter how extended the family.

There are only scant records of the good times and the bad times during Frederick's half century. History tells of a severe winter and ruined crops in 1816 which reduced many settlers to starvation and required a full decade to recover lost ground. By 1825, Pincombe (1969) states that one Peter Fisher reported:

Westmorland is silently enriching itself with the slow but sure returns of agriculture and fast rising in importance. But the most thriving class are the English, chiefly from Yorkshire and their descendants . . .

It was 1804 and ten of Frederick and Rachel's twelve children had been born before an enterprising gentleman from Lancashire,

John Bentley established a trading business along the Petitcodiac between Hillsborough and Monckton Bottom[1] (later Salisbury). In 1811, Bentley settled at The Bend to become its first merchant (Pincombe, 1969). Throughout Frederick's life, conditions changed little from frontier times; when he died (1830) there were only about 100 souls living at The Bend but great changes were not far distant since shipbuilding was just starting. Capt. Benjamin Stanton of Saint John built the first ship, the *Isabella*, on Hall's Creek (1826-27) and thus initiated the first boom on the upper Petitcodiac with the building of wooden ships (Pincombe, 1969; Larracey, 1985). Gradually, the days of barter and self-sufficiency would come to an end with the rise of an active industrial and business center in Moncton, providing abundant labor and bringing shops of all kinds, banks, newspapers, hotels, boarding houses, blacksmith shops, livery stables and taverns—referred to as "grog shops." But this was a different age, the times of great grandfather Ephraim and grandfather Stewart Alonzo.

THE DAYS OF EPHRAIM (1830-80)

Ephraim's times were boom times on the upper Petitcodiac. By 1855, the mid-point in his half century, The Bend had been incorporated as the town of Moncton [2] and the major shipbuilder Joseph Salter was elected its first mayor. One Moncton historian (Pincombe, 1969) refers to the period as the "Golden Age of the Fifties" while another terms it the "Fabulous Fifties" (Macum, 1965). Shipbuilding transformed The Bend from a village of about 100 in 1830 to a town of over 5,000 in 1880. During this period, the economy and social conditions changed forever along the Petitcodiac. The first bank at The Bend (Bank of Westmorland) was incorporated under an act passed 20 March 1854; a weekly newspaper *The Westmorland Times*, selling at 7s/annum appeared in 1855. By this time there was a ferry service across the river at Moncton (initiated by Simon Outhouse in 1841) but the first bridge was still more than two decades in the future (1867) and it survived only two years—destroyed by the Saxby Gale, the greatest natural disaster that ever hit the Petitcodiac.

The most active period of shipbuilding, which first put Moncton on the map, lasted between 1840 and 1875. The firm of G.&J.

Salter was the most active of several builders (Machum, 1965; Larracey, 1985). In all, about 40,000 tons consisting of 13 barques, 30 ships, one brig and other smaller vessels were constructed at The Bend; Salter's yard accounted for about half of the tonnage in the period 1847-57 employing 400 men at the peak in 1853. The largest ship to be constructed in Moncton was the *Lady Clarendon*—length 216 ft and tonnage 1,344. Most of these ships sailed away never to return, loaded with lumber for purchase in Britain, with Liverpool the most frequent destination. Shipbuilding at Moncton was only a part of the feverish construction at docksides all along the Petitcodiac from Alma and Riverside to Boundary Creek and Salisbury. Salisbury is at the head of tide and today one finds it hard to visualize the building of the large ships that went on there for forty years (1839-79). The *Petitcodiac*, a 146 ft 654-ton barque, launched in 1859, was the last ocean-going vessel to be built in Salisbury.

This feverish construction altered forever the character of frontier life on the upper Petitcodiac. Employment was abundant, not only in the shipyards but in the lumber woods and on the farms that fed the hungry men. The boom finished the cashless society and the days of barter. Hard cash was available for purchases of many services and items that would have been luxuries in Frederick's times. Banks and banking became facts of life. The Bank of Westmorland, Moncton's first bank failed in 1867 with the closure of Salter's shipyards but the Bank of Montreal (see Baskerville, 1987) opened on Main Street six years later(1873). The hard-working laborers quenched their thirsts and found relaxation in the taverns with the inevitable brawls of men loaded with too much rum. In 1855, Moncton got its first law officer, the town marshal Rufus Brown, who worked as a blacksmith in the yards by day and preserved law and order at night (Larracey, 1985).

Although there was a small flurry of shipbuilding between 1878 and 1882, the great days of wooden ships were over by 1861 when Moncton's population stood at 1,396. A decade of recession followed until, in 1871, Ottawa decided to locate the headquarters of the Intercolonial Railway in Moncton and the maintenance shops were opened in 1872. Prosperity returned but during the recession between ships and rails, many of our relatives left their homeland for the more prosperous climes of New England, especially Boston.

With the coming of railways in the 1870s, Moncton and the surrounding areas gradually turned their backs on the Petitcodiac; the arrivals and departures of vessels at Moncton's docks were less and less frequently in the news, even though some activity lived on into the first quarter of the twentieth century. In 1913, the year of my birth, exports from the Port of Moncton were valued at $496,379 and imports amounted to $911,030; molasses boats from the Barbadoes, in the early 1930s, were among the last of the regulars to discharge cargoes in Moncton (*The Times-Transcript* 8 September 1987). But long before this, regular passenger service which had connected the Port of Moncton with Saint John, Halifax and New England, was discontinued on the Petitcodiac while imports such as coal and exports like lumber moved on rails. With the completion of the causeway (1968) about two miles west of the great bend in the Petitcodiac, the upper part of the river became Petitcodiac Lake and the estuary at Moncton gradually filled with silt, ending the great tidal bores and eliminating all possibilities of water traffic between Moncton and the open Atlantic. The Port of Moncton is no more.

By the end of Ephraim's life, the city of Moncton was again busy and prosperous. With the emergence of a bustling rail center during the last part of the nineteenth century, several industries—now almost forgotten—developed: the Moncton Cotton Company (built 1882-83) employed 200 and turned out 12,000 yards of fabric per day; the Moncton Sugar Refining Company was a large operation near the Cotton Mill; later the buildings of the cotton mill became Marven's Biscuit Company and recently this has been converted into a one-stop home decorating center "The Factory." In the late 1800s, the Record Foundry was producing wood and coal burning stoves and furnaces and Peters Combination Lock Company had a thriving business but a short life (1880-83); the Peters establishment is now the Wallace Moving and Storage Company on Church Street (notes from *The Times-Transcript* 1987). When my mother was born (1881) and her grandfather Ephraim died (1883), Moncton was an active industrial center, a thriving place of business for the surrounding agricultural communities and the hub of the Maritimes with heavy rail traffic, connecting it with Upper Canada, the Canadian west and New England. Moncton's motto RESURGO was a reality (see *The Times-Transcript* October 1986).

51

Steeves Homestead (c1850). Attached building at the right was home in the early days of Ephraim—later a summer kitchen. Trees left to right: elm, maple and group of balm of Gilead.

As Ephraim and his family watched Moncton develop from a village into a city, they must also have seen their farm and the whole countryside change just as dramatically. The virgin forests were felled, sawed into lumber and hauled off to the dockside to be built into ships or loaded for markets in Europe (Lower, 1973; Wynn, 1985; Spicer, 1986). Many of the great trees were turned into lovely homes. The big white house, shown on the opposite page, was built about 1850 and it is most likely that the lumber used was harvested on the farm. The panelling on the ceiling of the living room is of 18 inch wide boards; the walls and ceiling of the kitchen of 12-13 inch boards; the bedroom panelling measures 8-9 inch; very large trees are required for long 18 inch boards. There were ready markets in Moncton not only for construction materials but for all sorts of produce to feed its expanding population or supply fodder for the horses in the livery stables. The local farmers became more and more prosperous as Moncton grew and the surrounding communities developed; self-sufficiency at the old homestead gradually disappeared with the change from barter days to a society that depended on hard cash.

I REMEMBER, I REMEMBER

> *Here from every doorway*
> *Looks a remembered face,*
> *Every sill and panel*
> *Wears a familiar grace.*
> *Bliss Carman (1861-1929)*

John Wesley was the fourth and last in the line of prosperous Steeves farmers who changed the wilderness lands in the Boundary Creek area into one of the most flourishing farms on the Salisbury Road. When I was a child the old homestead was probably at its peak of prosperity and, next to my own home, memories of the John Steeves household and its many relatives are clearest of all my childhood memories. Mother lived there until she was 31 and always felt a part of the place with a motherly interest in Uncle John and Aunt Celia's children and a feeling of involvement in the busy life there.

My brother and I remember it as a place that was always a step or a jump ahead of our dad's farm. There, we saw the most up-to-date farm machinery, big experiments with new cash crops (fox farming was a prime example), and a much greater range of agricultural products than at home; poultry included ducks swimming in the creek between the big barns and the house and turkeys in the barnyard; at home we had only hens and chickens. The same was true for other farm animals; there were usually 25-30 sheep and lambs—animals that I do not remember on other local farms—larger herds of cattle and so forth. At Uncle John's we heard the tinkle of the cream separator while at home we hung a "creamer" in the cool well. There we saw our first automobile at close quarters and listened to radio for the first time, if we could manage a turn at the ear phones. Uncle John evidently had his doubts about his brother-in-law, my dad, and put it thus:

> *More horses than cows*
> *More women than men*
> *He may get rich*
> *But Lord knows when.*

Dad made it in his own way and I am sure that Uncle John's banter was friendly. Of dad's many joys in life, a keen one was to drive west in the evening with mother beside him and Gerald and me on a small seat facing them behind the dashboard. In the summer, it was a four-wheeled buggy; in the winter a smoothly running cutter while we snuggled under a great buffalo robe and dozed off to the sound of sleigh bells in the crisp winter air.[3] While the grown-ups enjoyed a long evening of chitchat around the centrally-located wood stove in the old living room, we invariably went into our soundest of sleeps on the couch in the corner. I still remember the "trauma" of being pulled into outdoor clothes and bundled into the carriage or sleigh to continue our rudely interrupted sleep. There were many such trips (four miles there and four miles back) but the one I remember most clearly was homebound on a clear winter night when the sleigh turned over in a snow drift and I woke up to the sound of dad shouting "WHOA" as he raced down the road tightly holding the reins and trying to control the frightened horse. I was not amused and, for the life of me, could not understand my mother lying in the snow drift and having the laugh of her life. I now realize that her behavior was quite in character. The other clear memories of these trips are excited by the aroma of roasting turkey which greeted our arrival at Uncle John's on Christmas day—always linked to the sound of dad's "Merry Christmas" as he planted a Christmas kiss on Aunt Celia's lovely face. How many years did we spend Christmas there? Always, in my memory.

The family in mother's old home was a greatly extended one. I remember Aunt Celia most clearly for she seemed to be at the center of it all. Looking back after half a century, I feel that she would have been a truly remarkable lady in any age and any society. In my memories, the place revolved around her as she looked after the needs of her five grown up children—coming and going with their friends, the local school teacher, a stream of relatives always welcomed with outstretched arms, and a host of "hired men" to be fed and housed up the back stairs over the kitchen. The number of hired men could exceed a dozen in times of a "big push" such as construction of a new barn or the building of the big fox ranch. But there appeared to be a place for everyone, even the "tramp" with a designated room for him over the summer kitchen. Aunt Celia had some help from the older children and from a live-in lady Minnie Magee but she managed it all in the days before electricity, indoor plumbing, deep freezes and prepared foods. At one stage, I remember the daily baking of mountains of fox cakes when that activity was at a peak before the days of Purina Chow.

Grandfather Stewart Alonzo is also a part of my early memories of this old home. Details are not very definite since I write of the memories of a five year old recorded after a lapse of 70 years. There are others who remember him more clearly: a cousin, now a nonagenarian, remembers his reputation as a highly successful and prosperous farmer; my aunt who taught in the local school lived under the same roof for two years and recalls long evening chats when others of the family were out—perhaps at a turkey supper or a basket social; his quiet concerns and worries about different members of his family stand out in her memories. But his granddaughter Alberta who remembers him as a part of the family throughout her home life has told me most fully of her memories of seventy years ago. She remembers him as a man of few words who often ended his pronouncements with "So there!" In summary she writes:

55

I remember my grandfather so well; he was a sweet-dispositioned man. When he became ill he told my mother that he "didn't want to die and leave the little girls." Lillian and I were going to Business College in Moncton then. . . . We all loved him and respected him. His dog's name was Rover and he [Rover] could line up the cows and bring them across the railway track as well as any man and . . . always made sure of nipping the heels of the last cow in the barn. . . . Of course I never knew my grandmother and I think Aunt Nina [my mother] sort of filled that gap. She used to tell me "many a time I stopped the washing and made you candy to keep you from crying."

My scattered memories revolve about grandfather's large garden. He always seemed to be working there when we would arrive on a summer evening. To me, the garden was remarkable in having NO weeds and in producing vast quantities of all sorts of vegetables—sufficient to feed the large family household, with enough on the side for generous contributions to his son Albert's family after they moved to Moncton. I also see him with his thick white hair and beard sitting beside the cookstove in the kitchen with his dog Rover at his feet; it was there that mother went to talk with him while the others chatted in the living room. Gerald and I also remember his wood-working shop above the shed near the house; there we played in piles of shavings with all sorts of short ends of lumber for blocks. Finally, and quite clearly, I remember mother taking me to see him on his death bed when he gave me a gold coin because Stewart was a part of my name; the funeral and burial (Boundary Creek Cemetery) are also crystal clear probably because of my mother's grief.

Some of this grandfather lives on in an obvious way in my grandson Alex since he shares with grandfather Steeves and me the genetics of a color deficient male. The genetics is clear back to Jane Mitton but, as I shall tell later, her father's name is as yet uncertain. Either Alex or I might make the same mistake as grandfather Steeves did if we were sent to a drapery shop (probably dimly lighted) to buy a suitable black gown for a wife to wear to a family funeral; grandfather returned with one of bright purple; dark red would have been just as likely.

THE GHOSTS OF FREDERICK'S LANDS

Few families whose ancestors arrived in Canada in the mid-1700s have a more complete record of their early ancestry than the Steeves Family. Thanks to Esther Clark Wright, who has examined the archival material and studied the family traditions, there is: (a) an excellent historical study of the Petitcodiac River, telling the story of land settlement and the negotiations that brought Heinrich Stief, his family and friends to Monckton and Hillsborough Townships (Wright, 1945); (b) a detailed history of the Stief (Steeves) family in North America, their pioneer days in New Brunswick and the marriages, births and deaths of the seven sons and their progenies (Wright, 1961); and (c) a genealogical record of Heinrich and Rachel's many descendants through eight to ten generations (Wright, 1965).

Samphire Greens (1961) is still in print and lists the third Steeves generation (Heinrich and Rachel's grandchildren). My account which follows, lists Heinrich and Rachel's children with notes on their marriages and family sizes. Only the progeny of the fourth son, Frederick, will be traced with details of that branch of the family tree to which my mother belonged. In short, this book focuses on the generations that were born and grew to adult life on the old Frederick homestead located on the upper Petitcodiac River about eight miles west of Moncton. They are the ghosts that roam about the beautiful old home shown on page 52 and on the cover of this book. The summary of Heinrich and Rachel's family follows; five of the sons settled in Hillsborough while Christian and Frederick took up lands in Monckton Township.

(1) HEINRICH STIEF   M   RACHEL . . .
     c1730-78/80   c1749

JACOB (1750?-1803?) m 1772 Katharine or Catherine Lutz d 1827, daughter of the pioneer Michael Lutz; 4 sons, 2 daus.

JOHN (1752?-1821) m 1774 Margaret Lutz sister of his brother Jacob's wife Katharine; 10 sons, 2 daus.

CHRISTIAN (1753?-1820) m Rosanna Trites, daughter of the pioneer Jacob Trites (Treitz); settled in Monckton Township on the western portion of Heinrich's land grant; through this marriage, Christian also had title to a portion of Jacob Trites' lands at The Bend; 4 sons, 4 daus. Before her marriage to Christian, Rosanna had a daughter Elizabeth by Robert Cummings.

FREDERICK (2, see below)

HENRY (1758?-1826) m c1781 Mary Beck (1761-1826) daughter of Martin Beck who served in the Commissariat at Fort Cumberland; Martin Beck was of German or Polish descent; 4 sons, 1 dau.

LEWIS--LUDOVIC or LUTRICK (1760?-1827) m c1786 Elizabeth Porter (1770?-1850); 7 sons, 8 daus.

MATTHIAS (1761-1848) m Sophia Beck (1780?-1844), sister of his brother Henry's wife; tool maker and shipbuilder; 9 sons, 4 daus.

(2) FREDERICK STEEVES	M	(1) RACHEL SOMERS
1755-1830?	1781	b 1764
	1816	(2) ROSANNA TRITES
		(née RICKER)

Rachel was "sweet sixteen" when she wed Frederick—presumably in Hillsborough where they both lived. They settled on the eastern block of Heinrich's lands in Monckton Township and raised a dozen healthy children—the first generation to be born and grow up on the Frederick Steeves farmlands. All twelve children lived to marry and raise large families. Of Frederick, Heinrich and Rachel's fourth son, E.C.Wright (p. 50, 1961) says:

Frederick's [family] showed great vigour and the younger members of the family were as prolific and as competent as the older ones.

Nothing is known of the home life of this large family. Presumably, they lived in the part of the building shown at the extreme right of the sketch (p. 52). The family now refers to this as "the summer kitchen;" it was first located on a knoll ("the clay field") just west of its present location and moved when the large home was built in the days of Ephraim and Jane (about 1850). But perhaps Frederick and Rachel commenced their family life in a more modest log cabin like so many of the pioneers; perhaps

their first home was the old place occupied by Heinrich and Rachel in 1766 before the move to Hillsborough; perhaps it was
a reconstructed Acadian home. We do not know but it is agreed
that the "summer kitchen" was home when Frederick's son Ephraim
and his wife Jane ran the farm and when their first four or five
children were born. It was a typical pioneer home of the late
1700s with a large stone fireplace that served both to heat the
home and to cook food for the large family. There was a large
living area downstairs with a loft or attic for sleeping above.

Rachel died some time before her fifty-second birthday since
the records show that Frederick married Rosanna, widow of Jacob
Trites, on 16 January 1816. It seems that Rosanna predeceased
Frederick and there is a suggestion that Frederick spent his final
days in Salisbury, cared for by Mary Jaques (Chronology and Wright
p. 47, 1961). However, there are no certain records of the lives
of these progenitors or knowledge of their final resting places.
Again, quoting from Wright (p. 50, 1961):

> Frederick . . . had a Family Bible, and his family . . . display-
> ed a family cohesiveness which survived despite the weight
> of numbers and consequent wide dispersal of grandchildren
> and greatgrandchildren.

We have no record of a Family Bible in Frederick's household.
It might have been passed on to an older member of the family.
The only Family Bible known to our branch of the Steeves family
is that of Stewart Alonzo (fourth generation) and Amanda Colpitts
Steeves with entries in Amanda's neat handwriting. [4] However,
the Steeves Family Papers do include a beautifully lettered paper
recording the names and birthdates of Frederick's family. This
aged and much worn paper (see p. 60) suggests a pride in family
and is reminiscent of an early German "fraktur." Writing of the
German people in Pennsylvania, Ketchum (1957) says:

> The most widely known contribution of the Pennsylvania
> Dutch, of course, has been the outpouring of their creative
> fancies: painted chests, decorated barns, colorful household
> articles, slipware and sgraffito pottery, *fraktur* (illuminated
> writing elaborated with decorations drawn in color), and
> *Taufschine*—those lovely illustrated baptismal certificates.

Family of Frederick Steeves and Rachel Summers, married June 15th 1780. This beautifully-lettered paper, backed with loosely woven fabric, measures approximately 32x41 cm. It is now cracked and yellowed after a century among the Steeves Family Papers. Photo courtesy Jane R. Wood.

The Family of Frederick Steeves and Rachel Somers

ANDREW (1782-1846) m 1806 Elizabeth Smith (1782-1869); 8 sons, 2 daus.

HANNAH b 1783 m 1805 John Wortman; 3 sons.

LEWIS (1785-1859) m 1809 Elizabeth Trites; 1 son, 4 daus.

MOSES b 1787.

REUBEN b 1789 m 1813 Lydia Trites; 6 sons, 3 daus.

CHARLES (1791-1846) m 1813 Ruth Stiles; 6 sons, 5 daus.

JOSHUA (1793-1870) m 1817 Rosanna Jaques, a grandaughter of Christian (second generation); 5 sons, 6 daus.

ROSANNA b 1796 m 1815 John Lutz; 3 sons, 3 daus.

MARGARET (1800-68) m 1817 Charles Lutz; 5 sons, 9 daus.

NANCY (or ANN) b 1803 m 1826 John Jaques (grandson of Christian and brother of Rosanna who married Joshua above); John's mother Mary kept a tavern at Monckton Bottom (near Salisbury) and may have cared for Frederick in his last years as noted above.

EPHRAIM (3, see below)

DANIEL (1807-65) m 1828 Margaret Mitton, a sister of his brother Ephraim's wife; 5 sons, 7 daus. The Frederick farmlands were divided between Ephraim who inherited the homestead and the eastern part of the farm, and Daniel who inherited the western block—known as the Manzer Steeves place in my generation.

(3) EPHRAIM STEEVES	M	JANE MITTON
1805-83	1827	1808?-90

Ephraim and Jane were my great-grandparents and with their generation, the family history enters the memories of some cousins still living. There were good photographs taken in their time and their portraits, which hang in the parlor of the old homestead near those of mother's other grandparents,[5] indicate that they lived, loved and laughed like us. Even though life's routine has been changed forever by telephone, radio, TV, VCR and the endless rush of automobiles, they look like people with the same basic instincts, concerns and aspirations as the most of their descendants. They were not literate people for there were no rural schools in their childhood; they made "their marks" on legal documents and as Ephraim's will shows (Appendix B), they had a concern for each and every one of their many children. Both of Ephraim's parents and one of Jane's were Pennsylvania Dutch. Perhaps German was still spoken from time to time in the home.

Ephraim was a man of 22 years when he married Jane Mitton. Jane's home was on the Little River between Salisbury and Colpitts Settlement but her mother had grown up on a farm located about half way between Frederick's lands and The Bend. Jane probably visited her grandparents from time to time; there were many chances for meetings in the horse and buggy days. Besides, Daniel, Ephraim's youngest brother, had married Jane's sister Margaret the previous year and the families must have been very close. About 1830, Frederick divided his lands between Ephraim and Daniel.

Jane Mitton's ancestry links ours with the Trites family—another one of the Pennsylvania Dutch families that landed at Hall's Creek in June 1766. Jacob Trites (Treitz) and his wife Elisina had four children: Christian, Abraham, Jacob Jr., and Rosanna who married Christian Steeves. Jacob Trites, the pioneer, settled in what later became downtown Moncton and remained there when his compatriots moved to Hillsborough. Subsequently, when land grants were registered, Jacob received 2,190 acres extending west from Hall's Creek (Map p. 43).

Jane Mitton, our ancestor, came from Abraham's line. In 1790, he obtained a grant of 1,580 acres about four miles west of The Bend. He settled there with his wife who was Margaret Jones another of the young people who arrived on Captain Hall's ship in 1766. Their daughter Catherine became my great-great-grandmother through her marriage to Ralph Mitton. The farm where Catherine was born and grew to womanhood was located immediately west of the property that my grandfather Hoar purchased in 1890 (Hoar, 1985). In our generation it was known as the Andrew Steeves place. Originally, it was a strip of land over half a mile wide extending from the Petitcodiac River marshes north to Lutz Mountain. Interested descendants can easily find the property

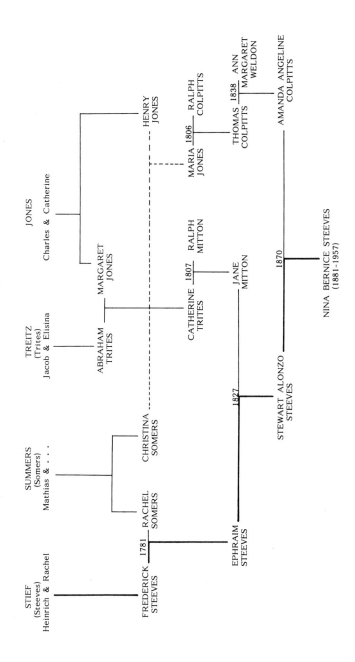

PENNSYLVANIA DUTCH CONNECTIONS

now since Fairhaven Cemetery is located on the western part of the old farm north of the Salisbury Road. In part, Abraham's grant (worded like many others of this period) reads:[6]

> George the Third by the Grace of God, of Great-Britain France, and Ireland, King, Defender of the Faith and so forth. To all to whom these presents shall come; Greetings: Know ye, that We, of our special Grace, certain Knowledge, and mere Motion, have given and Granted and by these Presents, for Us, our Heirs and Successors, do give and grant unto Abraham Trites his Heirs and assigns a Tract of Land situate, lying and being within the parish of Moncton (sic) in the county of Westmoreland (sic) and abutted and bounded as follows, to wit, beginning at a spruce Stake standing on the northerly bank or shore of Petcudiac (sic) river at the upper or southerly corner or bounds of a Tract of land granted to Michael Lutz . . . [follows survey data and details of boundaries] . . . saving and reserving to us our Heirs and Successors all mines of Gold Silver copper lead and Coals. To have and to hold the said Tract of one thousand five hundred and eighty acres of land . . .

On 3 February 1807, Catherine Trites married Ralph Mitton, a young farmer on the Little River a few miles south of Salisbury. Ralph was the adopted son of John Mitton (Mitten), a Yorkshire immigrant of 1774. John obtained a grant of 980 acres, immediately north of the Robert and George Colpitts holdings. Ralph's farm of 270 acres was located on the western boundary of his father's farm (Grant Index Plans No. 119 and No. 131, Dep't Natur. Resources and Energy, Crown Lands Branch, Fredericton, N.B.). Jane Mitton, my great-grandmother was presumably born there and would have been well acquainted with the Colpitts ancestors before she married Ephraim Steeves on 8 January 1827 and went to live in the Frederick Steeves homestead. To the genealogist, the interesting question concerns Ralph's natural father.

Wright (1978) records John Mitton's marriage to Elizabeth Johnson, a widow with a son Ralph who took the name of Mitton. W.B. Oulton [7] who has searched the census data, marriage bonds and records "suggests Stephen Johnson of Sackville the likely father" (letter dated 7 May 1987). But I also have a letter from

Waynes Johnston, [7] dated 25 April 1987 stating:

> Ralph was born in St. John in 1776 and died after 1851 as
> he is listed in that census—for Coverdale Parish. His father,
> a Blakely, was lost at sea. His mother Elizabeth, married
> John Mitton (1752-1834), who was a brother of my ancestor,
> William Mitton (b 1 April 1753).
> Ralph adopted the name Mitton. I am still trying to find
> out who Elizabeth Blakely was and where her first husband
> came from. She may have been a Johnson at one time...
> John Mitton came to Canada or N. B. in 1774 and settled
> near Sinton in Albert Co., . . . a few miles across the river
> from Salisbury . . . Elizabeth Blakely was a widow of Lan-
> caster or West St. John.

I have nothing further to offer concerning this great-grandmother's paternal ancestry—whether Johnson, Blakely or some
other. Great-grandmother Jane lived on for seven years after
Ephraim's death. His will (Appendix B) assured "his beloved wife
Jane Steeves in addition to her right of dower a suitable driving
horse and carriage and harness and farm things with sufficient
hay and pasture from year to year to keep them during her life."
My own mother would have been nine years old when her grandmother died and must have had many memories of her; sadly,
I never probed her memories of childhood. Perhaps she had some
happy rides in grandma's carriage with suitable driving horse.

The Family of Ephraim Steeves and Jane Mitton

ARCHIBALD b 1827 m 1858 Ann Lutz (1834-1919); settled on
Steeves Mountain; 4 sons, 11 daus. A daughter Delilah married
her cousin Bradford Mitton whose father Abram b 1821 was
Jane Mitton's brother. A grandson (Bradford C. Mitton) is a
source of information on the Mitton family. [8]

RALPH (1829-1903) m (1) Maria Jones (1835-73); 1 son, 3 daus.
m (2) Carolyn Jones; 2 sons, 2 daus. Ralph operated a livery
stable in Moncton. The youngest child of the second marriage
was Simeon who graduated from Mt. Allison University and
became a wealthy dentist in New York. The youngest daughter,
next older than Simeon, was a gifted pianist but died young
and was buried in the Wilson Cemetery just east of the Hoar

farm on the Salisbury Road. Her brother Simeon erected the most imposing monument in the cemetery in her memory and arranged annual care for the grave as long as he lived. Simeon married but there were no children.

NAOMI (1832-1903) m 1856 Israel Wilson (1827-97); 3 sons, 6 daus.

CATHARINE (1833-1910) m 1856 Abel Jones (1832-95), a farmer at Boundary Creek; 5 sons, 3 daus. The youngest son Cecil Charles was graduated in Mathematics from Acadia University and later became President of the University of New Brunswich (1906-40).

WESLEY (1835-1915), a bachelor remained on the homestead, assured in his brother's will of comfort there during his old age.

STEWART ALONZO (4, see below)

HANNAH (1839-47)

ROSANNA (1840-81) m 1869 Jordan Steeves (1836-1915), descendant of Matthias, youngest son of Heinrich and Rachel Stief. Rosanna and Jordan settled in Hillsborough where he ran a prosperous hardware shop. There were 3 sons, 3 daus. by this marriage and 1 son, 2 daus. by Jordan's second marriage to Catherine Wallace b 1855.

ADELINE b 1843 m 1878 James Charters; known in the family as Aunt Addie and Uncle Jim; 3 daus., the eldest Ella died at age 8 and is buried in the Wilson Cemetery. Aunt Addie ran a boarding house in Moncton until her daughters Ida and Addie went to Boston and found employment in the textile industry; the parents followed and established a home in Wakefield, Massachusetts.

BARBARA b 1845 m 1888 Roswell Colpitts descendant of Christian Steeves. No children.

ANDREW GILBERT (1847-1935) m c1875 Jane E. Jones (1848-1925). Uncle Andrew and Aunt Jane settled on the Abraham Trites property and raised one son Ralph C. (1877-1967) who inherited the farm and two daughters Alice (Swazy) and Jennie (Weldon). Aunt Jane was daughter of Charles Jones and Jane Mitton—two very familiar family names.[9]

The Ghosts of Frederick's Lands
ALMIRA JANE (1858-1919) m Stephen Bamford Weldon Colpitts
(1852-1925) a brother of Amanda Colpitts; 4 sons, 3 daus.
Stephen Colpitts was named for his uncle S.B.Weldon who farmed
the homestead in Coverdale (Sketch p. 90).

(4) STEWART ALONZO STEEVES 1837-1918	M 1870	AMANDA ANGELINE COLPITTS 1848-1901

When Amanda Colpitts married Stewart Steeves, she joined a
greatly extended family. Both of her husband's ageing parents
were still alive (Ephraim was then 65 years old); there were two
brothers-in-law, Wesley and Andrew and three sisters-in-law, Adeline, Barbara and [Almira] Jane; Jane, the youngest of Ephraim's
children, was then only 12 years old and one wonders what sorts
of stresses and strains developed during the early days of our
grandparents' honeymoon. Amanda is said to have been most like
her sister Aunt Annie Stevens whom many remember as a gentle,
thoughtful and lovely lady; perhaps all went smoothly. Initially,
it must still have been very much Ephraim's farm and Jane's
household.

As Ephraim aged, responsibilities for the farm gradually shifted
to Wesley and Stewart who remained on the farm after their
three brothers married and established homes elsewhere. Since
Wesley never married, the future of the farm was passed to Stewart whose title to the property was established in Ephraim's will
—dated 1882 (Appendix B).

Stewart and Amanda raised three children: John Wesley (1871-
1953), Nina Bernice (1881-1957) and Thomas Albert Colpitts (1884-
1940). During the ten year interval between the births of John
and Nina, a son Frank G.W. (1875-76) and a daughter Addie M.
(1878-79) died in infancy. Amanda had health problems for many
years and died at age 53 from what her generation termed "in-
flammation of the bowel;" this could have been any one of several
chronic conditions now well-known to the medical profession.
Because of her mother's ill health, my mother left school at
age 14 to help with the many duties in a large family home.

Amanda's prolonged illness created other problems. The manage-
ment of an extended pioneer family required mature decisions
almost hourly and plenty of hard work. About 1894, when my
mother left school, the situation became critical and John Wesley

67

(then in his early twenties) set out to find a housekeeper. He is said to have searched both sides of the river before he persuaded Celia Wortman of Upper Coverdale to take on the task. Celia, then in her mid-twenties, was home on holiday from Boston where she had been employed as a seamstress and later as a cook in a private boarding house. John must have been very persuasive for Celia would have been under no delusions concerning her many duties in the large farmhouse; Celia had left school at age 14 to manage her father's household when her mother died.

The "housekeeping" arrangement between John and Celia was of short duration; on 2 December 1895, John Wesley and Celia Maria were married—happily as I remember them.

In part, Celia's ancestry was also Pennsylvania Dutch. The Wortmans arrived in Monckton Township in 1766—probably on the same vessel as the Steeves, Trites, Somers and Jones ancestors, although this is not certain since their emigration arrangements were made through Clarkson and Company while the larger group signed on with Franklin and Company. After Celia's father Harding Wortman lost his first wife (Jane Kay) he married Jane Mitton widow of Charles Ayles. Of the several children born to Harding and Jane (Ayles) only Celia and a brother Herbert survived to adulthood; they had three half-brothers from their father's first marriage—Luther, Robert who drowned in the Petitcodiac and Jordan, called Uncle Jurd.

Celia's talents went far beyond those of most New Brunswick housewives. For example, at one stage in life she enjoyed painting, both on canvas and on velvet, and her daughter Alberta remembers her many trips to Moncton in the horse and buggy days for painting lessons while Aunt Nina kept things running smoothly in the farmhouse. Again, her skills in midwifery were known throughout the community and Alberta remembers frequent distress calls, often in the middle of the night, from local farmers and their wives; I have been told that I would never have known my mother had Aunt Celia been less knowledgeable in midwifery. I expect that Aunt Celia would have been an outstanding lady in any age and in any society.

John and Celia raised three sons and two daughters—listed in Appendix C; there was one infant death. With many other Steeves descendants from the times of Ephraim and Jane, John and Celia are buried in the Boundary Creek Cemetery.[10]

Stewart and Amanda's other two adult children, Albert and Nina, married the two eldest offspring of William C. Hoar and Carolyn L. (Newcomb). The history of the Hoar family was summarized in the first of this series of family history books (Hoar, 1985). When [Thomas] Albert, at age 21, married Minnie Hoar, Albert's father Stewart Alonzo established him on a farm directly to the east of the old homestead. Albert and Minnie's six children were born there before the family moved to Moncton and Albert found employment more compatible with his health than farming (Chronology and Appendix C).

Nina, my mother, spent the first 31 years of her life in her father's home. John and Celia's youngest child Louis was six years old when my mother married and, until the day of her death, she had a strong loyalty to her old home and a motherly love for her brother John's children.

Among the few written records that mother left is a pencilled diary (now rather tattered) of a trip that she and her father made to Woodstock (distance about 200 miles) where her Aunt Annie Stevens (Amanda's sister) lived. I quote a few paragraphs; they provide an intimate picture of travel in the horse and buggy days and speak volumes for hospitality in rural New Brunswick at the turn of the century.

> Father and I left home Tues. 10 [July] 1906 for Woodstock about 2 o'clock in the afternoon. We drove to Bruce Keith's to supper. Found no one home but the little girl Retta and the small children. But she got us a very nice supper. Then we drove over to Havelock. . . . Wed morning we started again . . . found a bad road right through the Canaan River. After crossing the Canaan River we had a long drive in a poor woody-looking country; took our lunch and Father fed the horse to oats and grass for an hour. . . . We drove. . . . till we struck a house this side of Chipman Crossing where we got supper at a Mr. and Mrs. Marr's, an old couple; their family had all left home. The charge was only 35 cts. We rested an hour and started on over a beautiful country along the shores of Grand Lake. . . . the horse got tired and we got tired and Pa stopped at a house. The lady told us she had company from Boston but perhaps her brother could take us in. So the brother said he would and he went

home with us. . . . there we found an old maid and batch and a little nephew. Mr. William Fanjoy and Miss Amy. Here we spent the night. Oh it was the loveliest spot I ever struck. Just like a dream. On the shores of Grand Lake. The lake is 18 miles long and from 4 to 6 broad. The beach was lovely; they keep the light house. Beautiful oaks. Father stepped one it was fifty feet across from branch to branch. The beach was so gravely and nice with bluebells and flags. There was a chance to dig freshwater clams and go boating. Mr. Fanjoy and I were going out but just like my luck it commenced to rain and my fun was over. . . . They would not take anything for our lodgings. Next morning we drove for Jemseg ferry 14 miles . . . The ferry seemed safe . . . just 30 miles to Fredericton . . . over the intervale we could see the river and sometimes over the river . . . a lot of barns and some old houses and an old church all uninhabited . . . It was a very pretty drive up to Fredericton . . . we crossed the river fed the horse an hour and look around. Stopped 14 miles up river to Mrs. McKeen's hotel . . . overnight. They charged us $1.15. . . . Had a nice drive and got here Friday night seven o'clock . . .

We left Woodstock on Monday morning after we were there a week and two days. Crossed . . . at Grafton and . . . found it settled right along and good roads. It commenced to drizzle rain about one o'clock and at four it just poured. . . . Father asked him if we might stand our horse in his barn and feed and get some supper. . . . they lived in the old Church of England parsonage . . . they didn't charge us anything for supper. . . . ferry across the St. John. The water was very deep and dark . . . it was a wire [cable] ferry. There were about six wire ferry down the river from Woodstock . . . and the charge was 15 cts.

On the return trip, they spent their first night in the hotel at Kingsclear and arrived in Fredericton on Tuesday morning. Nina reported that "it is prettier on the F'ton side of the river." The trip south on the west side of the St. John River seems to have been full of interest except for a monotonous detour "around two great bogs" and a slight disagreement with Pa who wanted to take advantage of a detour "but I pulled hard to go to Gagetown. I had very little intention of leaving the river.

So I had my way. Father was vexed and scolded but I saw Gage-town. It was only a little shipping place not near as nice as Salisbury." Points of special interst were the churches, "nearly all Church of England" and one with a spire "over a hundred ft." Westfield was noted as "a summer resort;" the Anagance woods did not seem to live up to its grim reputation and the comment was "I didn't mind the wood a bit as I expected." After they reached Saint John, they evidently enjoyed hospitality with relatives or acquaintances until they arrived in Boundary Creek. The final comment was "arrived home early Sat. evening; . . . Our expenses were just $8.05 cts.

Mother's generation had little leisure time or opportunity to travel but mother enjoyed her rare opportunities to the full. In our generation, she would probably have been an inveterate travel-ler. However, considering her times and place in society, she experienced some journeys that many only dreamed of. There were the occasional trips to Boston to visit the many cousins there—by overnight train in the horse-and-buggy days and later in the family car with a stop or two en route. The honeymoon to the Canadian National Exposition in Toronto and on to Niagara Falls was a highlight of her life. The local newspapers of the day give the setting for this happy event and departure for the ultimate in Canadian tours:

. . . wedding took place at the home of J.W.Steeves Salisbury Road at 4 p.m. on Tuesday Sept. 3rd, when his sister, Nina B. was united in marriage to George W. Hoar. . . . ceremony was performed beneath a floral arch erected on the lawn. . . . The bride, given away by her father, was becomingly gowned in cream duchess satin with veil of orange blossoms. [11] Her niece, Alberta Steeves, acted as maid of honor . . . The wedding march was rendered by Miss Lillian Steeves, niece of the bride. . . . There were about 150 relatives and friends present. . . . all repaired to the dining room where a sumptuous repast was served after which the happy couple left on the Maritime Express for Toronto, Niagara Falls and other Canadian points amid the good wishes of their many friends.

With the wedding at 4 p.m. it is obvious that night had come long before the happy couple was able to depart. According to Uncle Rob who drove them to the station in Moncton, the night was so black that he could hardly see the tail end of the driving horse. As I remember, the Maritime Express departed about midnight.

Finally, in the autumn of 1953, mother had her first taste of aeroplane travel when she crossed the continent in one of the old North Stars. Air travel was then coming into its own in a big way but jets were still in the future. Of her trip to Vancouver, she wrote to a long-time friend:

> It is so nice to be here . . . flowers and trees everywhere. Some of the older homes have so many trees one would think they lived in a forest. . . . it was a grand trip so much nicer than train . . . between Toronto and Winnipeg the plane got very warm and there was an electric storm. But most of the time it was the same as when you were with me. . . . The lights of Montreal and Toronto were grand and we got a splendid view of the cities high up. The prairies look like oilcloth. Blocked off in green, brown and yellow; the homes like play houses; the cars like bugs; telephones like clothes lines; the clouds like soap bubbles with sky above; the mountains like crystal with trees, cracks and rivers with some snow. Guess the sun made them so shiny. I never thought the mountains would be so grand. The rivers and lakes were so blue; trees on mountains—at first I thought it was moss but as we got lower one could easily see it was trees.

REFERENCES

Baskerville, P.A. 1987. Banking on it. Horizon Canada 10(112): 1672-2677.

Hoar, W.S. 1985. Branches of a family tree. The Hoar ancestry. Tangled Roots, Vancouver. 52 p.

Ketchum, R.M. 1957. Fast clocks, plain food and "fraktur." "The American Heritage Book of Great Historic Places." pp. 120-121. Am. Heritage Pub. Co./Simon and Schuster, New York.

Larracey, E.W. 1985. Chocolate river. Lancelot, Hantsport, N. S. 254 p.

Lower, A.R.M. 1973. Great Britain's woodyard: British North America and the timber trade, 1763-1867. McGill-Queen's Univ. Press, Montreal. 271 p.

Macum, L.A. 1965. A history of Moncton town and city 1855-1965. Moncton Pub. Co., Moncton, N.B. 447 p.

Pincombe, C.A. 1969. The history of Monckton Township (CA. 1700-1875). Thesis Univ. New Brunswick. 339 p. [Microfilm No. 5694. NL-101 (1/66). Nat. Library of Canada.]

Spicer, S.T. 1986. Shipbuilders to the world. Horizon Canada 5(52): 1225-1231.

Wood, R. (ed.) 1942. The Pennsylvania Germans. Princeton U.P., Princeton, N.J. 299 p.

Wright, E.C. 1945. The Petitcodiac. Tribune Press, Sackville, N.B. 76 p.

Wright, E.C. 1961. Samphire greens. The story of the Steeves. Author Publication, Wolfville, N.S. 109 p.

Wright, E.C. 1965. The Steeves descendants. Author Publication, Wolfville, N.S. 923 p.

Wynn, G. 1985. Hail the pine. Horizon Canada 4(37): 872-877.

Steeves Family Logo

MONCKTON LANDS OF HEINRICH STIEF
A Chronology through Eight Generations

1766

Heinrich and Rachel Stief with their seven sons landed at the mouth of Panacadie (Hall's) Creek on 3 June. The family settled about eight miles west
of The Bend on lands north of the Petitcodiac River in the region of Island
Creek. At this time Frederick, the fourth son, was about eleven years old.

1769-70

After three very lean years, the Stief family moved to Hillsborough Township
where, with adequate logistic support, their fortunes steadily improved.

1778

Through the Courts of Nova Scotia, Heinrich brought suit against absentee
landlords in Philadelphia, seeking damages and land title in Monckton Township
for breach of terms of the land settlement agreement. Suit was successful
and Heinrich was awarded damages, costs and 2,163 acres of marsh and upland
in the Island Creek area.

1780

Title to Monckton lands recorded in Cumberland County Records and later confirmed when New Brunswick became a separate province in 1784.

1778-80

Death of Heinrich followed by family decision to divide the Monckton lands
between Christian and Frederick. Christian took title to the western parcel
of 1,159 acres while Frederick settled on 1,034 acres to the east.

1780

Frederick married Rachel Summers (Somers); they settled on the Monckton lands
and raised 12 children. After Rachel's death, Frederick married (1816) the
widow of Jacob Trites, Jr., who was born Rosanna Ricker.

1827

Ephraim, Frederick's eleventh offspring, married Jane Mitton; they raised
12 children; my grandfather Stewart Alonzo, the sixth child, was born in
1837. Daniel, Frederick's youngest child married Jane Mitton's sister Margaret
and they also raised 12 children.

1829

Ephraim and Daniel paid Henry Jones 110 pounds for a parcel of land on the
eastern boundaries of Frederick's farm; this land was added to the Frederick
farmlands (boundaries recorded in Steeves Family Papers).

1830-34

A Steeves Family Paper dated 8 May 1834 reads: "Whereas one Frederick Steeves
late of Monkton [sic] in the county aforesaid in and by his last Will and

74

testament bearing date the seventh of May in the year of our Lord one thousand eight hundred and thirty did amongst other things devise unto his sons Daniel Steeves and Ephraim Steeves jointly all that tract of land in the Parish of Monkton where he then resided together with three small . . . of marsh in Coverdale subject to his widow Rosannah Steeves claiming her third or right of dower . . . [In 1816, after the death of his first wife, Frederick married Rosanna (Ricker) Trites, who predeceased him. There is a suggestion that Frederick spent his last days in Salisbury with a relative Mary Jaques who ran a tavern there (Wright, p. 47, 1961). A paper with a Salisbury dateline 28 February 1831 refers to the making of a coffin which was probably Frederick's—suggesting further that he may have died in Salisbury.]

Frederick's farm was divided between Ephraim who inherited the homestead and the eastern part of the original farm while Daniel farmed the western half—property known in my youth as "the Manzer Steeves Place." Manzer was Daniel's grandson.

1836

Weekly stagecoach service between Saint John and Amherst, passed along the highway in front of the Steeves homestead every Tuesday morning en route to Amherst and again on the return trip Wednesday evening.

1837

Birth of Stewart Alonzo Steeves. Several elder family members hold that grandfather Steeves was born in the recently-constructed new home (p. 52) which is said to have been built between the births of Catherine (1833) and Stewart. Another tradition places construction of the home at a later date with memories that the home was built the year the rail service was established between Boston and Halifax; since trains did not run between Saint John and Moncton until 1860 this tradition, if correct, means that Stewart was born in the old part of the house ("summer kitchen"). But perhaps it was the year of stagecoach service from Saint John (1836) rather than rail service. Two facts are definite: (a) the big barn was built in 1869 with reconstruction in 1914-18 and (b) the house does not bear a Centennial Plaque; Centennial Plaques were placed on all New Brunswick homes built in 1867 or earlier; however, this may mean only that the date could not be established at the time of the centennial survey.

1840-75

The great days of shipbuilding on the upper Petitcodiac River, especially at The Bend but also in Boundary Creek and Salisbury where the first ship was built in 1839.

1855

The Bend becomes the town of Moncton, incorporated 12 April. Moncton became

75

a city in 1890.

1860

First railway train from Saint John to Moncton passed the Steeves homestead on 1 July (European and North American Railway). Trains carried mail from this time.

1870

Stewart Alonzo, my grandfather, married Amanda Angeline Colpitts in Pleasant Vale on 31 December.

1871

New Brunswick School Act provides for free nonsectarian education. Sometime thereafter a small one-room school was opened about one mile east of the Steeves homestead; here, three generations of Steeves children received their primary education. A class photograph taken beside the school c1895 shows a teacher with 14 pupils including my mother and her brother Thomas Albert. The school must have been at capacity. When my Aunt Ethel (née Baird) taught there in 1914, only six pupils attended—the four younger children of the Steeves family and two Tingley children.

1883

Ephraim died on 25 October. Stewart inherited the family farm ". . . I give devise and bequeath to my son Stewart Steeves all the rest and residue." Ephraim's last will and testament was dated 31 March 1882.

1892

Methodist Church built about one mile west of the Steeves homestead on land once a part of Christian's holdings. Foundation laid 4 April; church dedicated 10 July on the site where William Black first held services in a tent in 1781. The spire of this church was topped by a closed right hand with forefinger pointing to Heaven; this spire was destroyed by lightning and replaced by a bell tower.

In 1939, the church was moved about eight miles east along the Salisbury Road, enlarged and officially named "Steeves Memorial."

Grandmother (Amanda Colpitts) is said to have been a prime mover in the establishment of the original church, bemoaning the fact that her children were growing up in a churchless community. Grandfather Stewart in the horse-and-buggy days, went to Charlottetown for the chandelier—an ornate fixture bearing many oil lamps that hung in the middle of the church; grandfather's selection disappeared when the church was moved and electrified; it probably rests in some long-abandoned garbage fill.

1895

John Wesley, eldest son of Stewart and Amanda, married Celia Maria Wortman on 2 December. John continues big-time farming and in his father's later

76

years inherited the homestead and his share of the farmlands.
1905
Thomas Albert Colpitts Steeves, Stewart's son married Minnie E. Hoar and was settled by his father on the "Mugridge Place" located near the eastern boundary of the Frederick property. The Mugridge Property included a large shuttered house just north of the highway and two barns across the road to the south. Albert and Minnie's six children were born in this house where the family lived until Albert gave up farming because of rheumatism and built a home in Moncton (302 High Street), where Albert was employed by Frost and Wood Farm Machinery Company; later he became a postal clerk on trains between Halifax and Montreal in the days when mail was sorted en route between major cities.
1912
A Steeves Family Paper dated 11 May states the boundaries of the two properties when Stewart Alonzo divided his lands between his two sons—John W. and Thomas Albert. Without going into the matter in detail, we feel that the division was probably about equal with John receiving the western half with the homestead and Albert the eastern half where the Mugridge home was located; Stewart may have retained some acreage himself.
1918
Death of Stewart Alonzo of the fourth Steeves generation on 3 October. His son John's faithful diary records (3 October):"Father died this morning at 1:10. He was a great sufferer with the exception of the last two days. He was 81." And again on 6 October: "Very stormy disagreeable day heavy rain all day . . . and this afternoon father was buried . . . was very large funeral considering the day and heavy rain."
1922
Front of family home altered by addition of stone porch (see front cover).
1953
Death of John Wesley (intestate) marking the end of the era of "big time farming" by Frederick's descendants. By this time, John's eldest son Weldon had a home in Salisbury where he was a shopkeeper; the second son Stewart was in business as a merchant in Gunningsville (Riverview); Louis, the youngest son, operated the farm during his father's last years but, subsequently, was employed by the Highways Department and in 1961 moved with his family to Salisbury.
1961
Stewart A. of the sixth generation purchased the farm from his brother Louis and commenced some work of restoration; he was raising beef cattle at the time of his death from a heart attack on 30 April 1964.

77

Steeves and Colpitts Pioneers

1964
Audrey (Gaskin) Steeves, widow of Stewart A., inherited the Steeves property.
1972
Farm sold to Louis Richard who also farms the Daniel lands to the west, thus uniting most of the original Frederick lands in one farming operation. Audrey retained title to the old home and five acres of land nearby.
1977
Title of old Steeves home and associated five acres of property jointly held by Audrey Steeves, her daughter Catherine Wood and her granddaughter Jane Ruth Wood. Jane lives in the ancestral home (1988) and maintains a small garden near where I remember my grandfather, with his great shock of snow white hair and beard, standing tall among the pole beans and corn.

2.5 cm

Plant of Goose Tongue

78

4

THE YORKSHIRE SETTLERS

Michael Francklin (1720-82) was responsible for the immigration of eleven boatloads of Nova Scotia settlers, totalling well over 1,000 persons. Most of them came from Yorkshire. The first group sailed from Liverpool on the *Duke of York*, 16 March 1772 and landed at Halifax 46 days later, whence they trans-shipped to Fort Cumberland, arriving there 21 May. The American Revolution brought this migration to an end.

Francklin himself was a wealthy business man and an astute politician who exercised enormous influence over the Acadians and the Micmacs. He served as Lieutenant Governor between 1766 and 1768 and proved to be wise and popular. Arriving in Halifax in 1752, Francklin set up a rum shop and began to amass a fortune trading in wine and spirits and supplying the naval and military stores during the Seven Years' War. Later, in the critical years of the American Revolution, he became the most powerful single influence in Nova Scotia (Kerr, 1934).

Francklin's political, business and social connections enabled him to obtain large acreages of excellent farmlands in the days when lands were readily available after the Expulsion of the Acadians. He took full advantage of his opportunities and attempted to fulfill his dreams of becoming a great landlord by acquiring large blocks of land on the Isthmus of Chignecto. Land speculation becomes profitable only when the lands are settled by productive farmers, and, by 1770, Francklin was "land poor." He and his associates, who were strong British loyalists, turned to the motherland for settlers. They were well aware of the general unrest and anxiety for the future created throughout Britain by the Industrial and Agrarian Revolutions.

While in England in 1769 settling some financial affairs, Francklin contacted the Duke of Rutland, many of whose Yorkshire tenants were having problems paying their rents. Subsequently, the Chignecto lands were advertised and promoted systematically throughout Yorkshire and attracted great interest among both rich and poor. The advertised lands seemed almost unbelievable in requiring no manure, while the terms of settlement were most remarkable:

> A man may have as much land as he pleases; the first year he pays nothing; for the next five years a penny an acre; the next five, three pence; and then one shilling an acre forever to him and his heirs. See Brebner p. 114 (1937).

Although the number of Yorkshire settlers was relatively small when compared with the influx of pre-loyalist New Englanders or many later emigrations to Canada, this influx had a far greater impact than many migrations of much larger magnitude. Two main factors were important. First, many of the migrants were persons of means who came with financial resources to purchase land and establish homesteads. One of the first arrivals, Charles Dixon, purchased 2,500 acres of land in Sackville and moved there with his family; both William Black and Robert Colpitts, among mother's ancestors, undertook preliminary journeys "to spy out the land" before committing their families to an arduous sea voyage and pioneering life under primitive conditions; William Black, having satisfied himself about the future possibilities, purchased an estate, returned to England to bring his wife, five children, a nurse maid, some improved breeds of cattle and the family possessions; Robert Colpitts' return trip is detailed in a later section. Most of these settlers were persons of strong moral character and often converts of John Wesley who, at an early stage in his ministry, had brought his message of salvation to Yorkshire; they were the founders of Methodism in Canada and, at a later date (1839), one of their number established Mount Allison University.

Further, the impact of the Yorkshire settlers on the farming methods of the colony cannot be overestimated. The Acadians had practised the time-honored European farming methods of the middle ages, cultivating the land with hoe, shovel and primitive plow; the productivity of the Acadian lands depended on the fertilizing wealth of the Fundy tides. The New Englanders who followed the Acadians were usually merchants and small-time farmers who learned the tricks of marshland cultivation from the remnants of the Acadian population. Travellers to Nova Scotia in the eighteenth century were not impressed by the farming methods of either the Acadians or the New Englanders; in general, crops were limited and productivity low. In contrast, the Yorkshire men—as a result of the Agricultural Revolution in England—brought to Eastern Canada the most advanced farming methods of their times. These included: cultivation of large fields devoted to a single crop, crop rotation, the use of artificial fertilizers, improved farm machinery (Tull's seed drill, cultivators, new plows), and improved breeds of farm animals. At a somewhat later date, annual county fairs, and farm magazines helped to disseminate information and promote competition for improving agriculture.

It is also important that the success of these Yorkshire farmers greatly altered thinking in the homeland with a positive effect on subsequent emigration to Canada.

> . . . their success in the new country as farmers and settlers forever removed from the English mind the belief that Nova Scotia was a cold, barren and inhospitable country, "fit only as a home for convicts and Indians." And thus it opened the way for future settlers. . . . Industrious, hardy, resourceful and God-fearing, they were made of the right material to form the groundwork of prosperous communities, and wherever this element predominated it was a guarantee that justice and order would be maintained (Trueman, p. 49, 1902).

Yorkshire men and women were among the most dedicated of pioneers. They were staunchly British, living in a colony largely settled by pre-Loyalist New Englanders who were hotly debating the question of independence from the motherland. A cairn at Fort Beauséjour (Fort Cumberland to the English colonists) recognizes their contribution to the region and the nation.

YORKSHIRE IMMIGRATION

Between 1772 and 1776 many settlers came to Chignecto from Yorkshire, England, owing to the efforts of Lieutenant Governor Michael Francklin. During the American Revolutionary War their loyal support of the authorities helped to quell the Eddy Rebellion of 1776. Their descendants have been prominent in the development of the country.

THE EDDY REBELLION

Jonathan Eddy settled in Cumberland, coming from Mansfield, Massachusetts with his family in 1759. He had strong loyalties to the cause of independence and over a two-year period (1775-76) attempted to create an uprising of Nova Scotia settlers that would bring the colony into open revolt with the British. Eddy received encouragement but virtually no material support; George Washington and Congress regarded Nova Scotia as peripheral to the central action and realized that without naval strength to match the British, there was little chance of either taking Nova Scotia or holding it.

At last Eddy, pushing the cause in New England, became impatient and acted on his own. Based on what he considered evidence of support in Cumberland, Saint John and Cobequid, he raised a small group of 72 raiders in Machias, Passamaquoddy and Maugerville. In the autumn of 1776, Eddy and his small force sailed up the Bay of Fundy in small boats, looting several places and intimidating the inhabitants. By the time they reached Fort Cumberland, about one hundred of the local New Englanders and Acadians had joined the cause. The Commandant of Fort Cumberland settled down to wait for support and the raiders, who lacked artillery and discipline, satisfied themselves with local raids; Eddy dispatched messages to Boston appealing for aid while the commandant at the Fort sent urgent pleas to Windsor for reinforcements. Brebner (1937) regards the whole affair as amateurish and disorganized. After about three weeks, two companies of Marines under Major Batt and Captain Studholm ended the farce; the besieging force was surprised and fled in disorder. ". . . gradually affairs quieted down. Eddy's men and true sympathizers found their ways back to Maine where some of them joined in the attempts to make war on the new frontier, the St John valley. Nova Scotia was never again during the Revolution in even as little danger as during November 1776" (Brebner, 1937).

The assessment of one of the Yorkshire farmers in a letter to the homeland is quoted from Bird (1948):

> There has been trouble here with Maine men and some Indians pretending to be an army to take the fort. They raided the homes of about twelve families in Sackville, taking most

83

of Mr. Dixon's supplies for the winter. They even came to Mr. Chapman's at Fort Lawrence and took his butter and geese. But at the Point and in Maccan we let them know we had no fowl or meat to be taken without payment and they soon slunk away. We wish no harm to any and will have none of the quarrel but what we have raised we will keep safe unless they who come have money to pay for their needs.

We have had some trouble with raccoons in our buckwheat fields and have lost seven sheep, killed by six bears, but have prospered nevertheless and are thankful we have come to this country.

Your brother

Silas

The rebellion led by Jonathan Eddy in 1776 receives scant attention by historians of the period—a small episode in the bitter War of Independence from which the United States of America emerged with the Treaty of Paris in 1783. None the less, Eddy's attack, poorly manned and badly organized, was the only actual invasion of the colony and, had the Cumberland settlers been sympathetic, a nasty revolt might have occurred. Many writers agree that it was the staunch attitude of the Yorkshire settlers that discouraged a general uprising (Godfrey, 1985). W.F.Ganong in the Introduction to Trueman (1902) writes:

> While it is doubtless too much to say that their loyalty saved Nova Scotia (then including New Brunswick) to Great Britain by their steadfastness at the time of the Eddy incident of 1776, there can be no doubt that it contributed largely to that result and rendered easy the suppression of an uprising that would have given the authorities very great trouble had it succeeded. But there can be no question whatever as to the value to the Chignecto region, and thence to all parts of Canada, of this immigration of God-fearing, loyal, industrious, progressive Yorkshiremen.

The cairn at Fort Beauséjour is a fitting recognition of their loyalty to the motherland. Thomas H. Raddall weaves the story of the Eddy Rebellion into *His Majesty's Yankees*, a historical novel of these stirring times.

84

TO SEEK A BETTER LIVELIHOOD

In this five-word phrase, Robert Colpitts recorded his reasons for migrating to Nova Scotia. The same reason was given by more than fifty percent of the heads of households who travelled with our Yorkshire ancestors in the emigrations of 1774-75. Although these emigrants came from many walks of life, the majority registered themselves as farmers or husbandmen. They were young (mostly not more than 30 years of age) and their mass emigration shows that they had little confidence in the future of farming as a way of life—not because farming was no longer a successful venture in mid-eighteenth century Britain but because of profound changes brought about by the enclosure acts and the introduction of new farming methods. In fact, farms were becoming progressively more productive and the land owners more prosperous with new crops and improved breeds of livestock. At the same time the yeoman farmers and the peasantry had become less and less secure. In earlier centuries while much of the land was held in common, subsistence living was guaranteed for most; with the improved methods of farming and the accelerated redistribution of the land, many found that there was no longer a place for them in the sleepy hamlets and villages of the English countryside. Emigration was seen as an inviting road to a "better livelihood." The forces that sparked many of these migrations are found in the Agricultural Revolution.

ENGLAND IN THE 1700S: A CENTURY OF PROFOUND CHANGE

For centuries, farming was the main occupation in Britain, providing work for all—even though the labors were not efficiently organized. The time-honored agricultural method was "strip farming" where a farmer's land was scattered in many small strips over several large village fields; fields were cultivated according to a plan agreed to by all with a third of the land lying fallow each year. There was no rotation of crops and, without fertilizers, the land became less and less productive. Coupled with this were the traditional methods of planting by broadcasting the seed and leaving Mother Nature to take care of it until harvest. Yields were scant and the quality of the food was inferior.

Early in the eighteenth century, Jethro Tull introduced his seed drill and horse hoe. He promoted the planting of seed in rows or in fenced fields devoted to a single plant species. These new farming methods resulted in steady crop improvements. Increased productivity of livestock also followed the abandonment of archaic practices. In earlier times, domestic animals were pastured on a village "common" where one farmer's cattle and sheep mingled with those of his neighbors, resulting in a community gene pool and precluding breed improvements.

By the early years of the century it was becoming clear that larger land owners, who may have acquired their holdings through astute marriages or otherwise, were out-producing the village farmers at an astonishing rate. Large fields devoted to a single crop and planted with the new machines together with proper rotation of crops, permitting the use of all the land every year, were steadily increasing the quality, the quantity and the variety of foods. At the same time, selective breeding and the isolation of farm animals was producing far more dairy products, meat and wool. For example, the average weight of oxen at Smithfield in 1710 was 370 lbs but 800 in 1795 while comparable figures for calves were 50 lbs vs 150 and for sheep 38 lbs vs 80 (Plumb, (1963).

Realization that wealth, power and prestige came with large land holdings foreshadowed the end of strip farming and the village common. Even though there might be great poverty for some, the powerful land owners were bound to succeed in their drives for large estates while the independence of hundreds of small farmers disappeared. The basis of these changes was the Enclosure Movement which started in the days of Queen Anne (1702-14) and reached its peak in the times of George III, during whose reign 3,200 enclosure acts were obtained with a General Enclosure Act in 1801 that simplified the procedures (Derry and Jarman, 1979). In brief, this movement created large farms out of the scattered strips of earlier days; unless a man had legal proof of his rights (unlikely in a society that had been relatively stable for many generations) his land was relocated or lost to make way for the big farms and the more efficient methods of farming.

Associated with these changes in land use was a steady growth of population after about 1740. This was less the result of increased productivity of the land than a decline in the death rate with

86

improved midwifery, and the foundation of lying-in hospitals and orphanages. With all these changes, there was a rapidly expanding middle class that no longer had the capacity to produce its food. Moreover, game laws were becoming ever more stringent and the possibilities of living off the land ever more remote.

The eighteenth century was not only a time of great social changes on the home front but also a century of profound political shifts in the world arena: the Seven Years' War (1756-63) that settled the conflict between England and France in America gave Britain a vast new land to colonize and develop; the American Revolution (1775-83) resulted in another English-speaking nation with different political allegiances and, finally, in the closing years of the century, the French Revolution (beginning in 1789) literally created a new world order in Europe, altering political systems and having far-reaching consequences in economics, religion, legal and educational systems extending far beyond the French Republic.

Out of this social and political upheaval, our Yorkshire ancestors appeared on the Isthmus of Chignecto ready to establish new homes in a new land. They answered the challenges of their times by emigrating but they were very few of the many whose lives were dislocated by the agrarian revolution. Thousands left the land to operate the new machines in textile and other factories; many went to the mining towns or became involved in the big boom of building roads and canals—all a part of the Industrial Revolution going on at the same time as the Agricultural Revolution. Towns expanded and great cities like Birmingham, Leeds and Manchester appeared while the villages of previous centuries were deserted, as Oliver Goldsmith wrote in the *Deserted Village*:

> . . . *a bold peasantry, the country's pride,*
> *When once destroyed can never be supplied.*

Did our Yorkshire ancestors make the right choice? Probably. The four families linked in mother's ancestry prospered in south-eastern New Brunswick, became persons of influence in shaping the future of the Maritimes and, later, saw their family names established widely throughout North America. A letter from William Colpitts of Streatlam, England written to his brother Robert in Hillsborough, Westmorland County, New Brunswick seems relevant. The letter, dated 29 April 1800 (17 years after the Colpitts family emigrated), read as follows:

Dear Brother:-

I received your letter with power of attorney, dated Jan. 7th, 1799, on 2nd Aug., Halifax postmark May 31st. I have a most melancholy tale to relate to you, as we have every appearance of famine both for man and beast. We have had the wettest harvest I have ever known. Many a poor farmer scarcely has corn to seed and bread them. What little wheat I have sold lately 14s 6d per bushel. Old corn at 25s per bushel; butter 1s 6d, oats, new 6s-4d per bushel. I have never heard of any barley being made into malt. We have had a very severe winter thus far, and I am afraid my fother [fodder] will be gone by Lady Day [25 March].

You make mention in your letter of your expectation of seeing your native country. God grant that I may see you again in it, but I think it has neither health, peace or plenty. Mrs. Lee has corn out on barn and castle moor, in Feb. 4, and I suppose about Lanchester, there is corn out and uncut yet on Ash Wednesday.

Dear Brother, I am very glad to learn of your son Thomas' marriage to Eunice Reynolds, and am glad of their going to their own farm as we can do no such thing here.

Every township is taking precaution to provide for the poor, and those that have no relief have what they call soup-kitchens. Beef is boiled in water with potatoes, peas and oatmeal, and boiled until it has the consistency of good broth and sold to the poor at a penny a quart, with a biscuit.

Hay got a shilling a stone [14 lbs] last year, and wheat to 4s a sheave. Many herd of cattle died last year for want of fodder. I was in Darlington on the first Monday in March, and barley was selling at 10s per bushel, mutton at 6d per pound, fall beasts 7d per stone.

We had it in the newspapers of great damage done at Halifax in Nova Scotia, by the great sea and floods, as you mention.

Oh, that I had gone with you to America! As I am fully persuaded that a man that wishes to be honest can never obtain a livelihood here. Nothing is to be seen here but cheating, tricking, fraud, oppression and selfishness; for if a man can get money by any means, only keep his neck out of the halter, he is reckoned a sensible, wise man, and looked up to by everybody.

This is the saddest war that ever England was engaged in, and God knows when it will have an end, for there is no sign of peace as yet.

I must conclude this long letter with hopes that it will find you and all your children in health and in peace and plenty, and for God's sake, come over if it is possible, and in the meantime, I subscribe myself,

Your loving brother
William Colpitts.

Streatlam, Eng.
29 April 1800

YORKSHIRE CONNECTIONS

Yorkshire people form four main branches of my mother's family tree. Her mother, Amanda Colpitts, was directly descended from William Black, William Chapman, John Weldon and Robert Colpitts, emigrants to Canada in 1774 and 1775. The Chapman and Weldon families were among the 187 passengers who sailed from Hull on the *Albion*, 14 March 1774; William Black with his family and Robert Colpitts who travelled alone, sailed from Hull in a group of 81 emigrants on the *Jenny*, 9 April 1775. William Black had visited Nova Scotia earlier and purchased property before returning for his family. Robert Colpitts returned to England after satisfying himself concerning a future in Nova Scotia but was unable to bring his family until the end of the Revolutionary War (1783). The intermarriages of these four families are shown in the chart p. 130. Following are some notes on their backgrounds and emigrations.

WILLIAM BLACK, b 1732 in Paisley, Scotland was the son of a public official who possessed an independent fortune. In his early yers, William lived a life of leisure doing "little else than the recreation of the hounds." At 21 years of age, he became

Weldon Homestead in Coverdale
John Weldon and Mary (Chapman) Weldon m 1806

90

a travelling salesman for a large manufacturing company, met and married (c1758) Elizabeth Stocks (b c 1739) in Huddersfield, England where he was engaged in the linen and woollen drapery business. Mrs. Black, like her husband, came from a wealthy family and "moved in the higher circles of fashion and refinement. She was accustomed to follow the hounds. When she came to Nova Scotia, she brought the scarlet riding habit and cap she used to wear when engaged in the chase; also, dresses of embroidered white satin and other rich and costly materials for which she found little use in the new country" (Black, 1885).

In 1772/74 William Black journeyed to Cumberland, purchased land in Amherst and returned to England for his family. [1] He and his family are listed among the passengers of the *Jenny* (1775). The ship list records his profession as a linen draper and gives his age as 43. Five children are listed; Sarah, our ancestor, was then seven. Mrs Black was injured in Halifax while embarking for Cumberland and died of her injuries a year later.

After his second marriage, William Black purchased a large estate in Dorchester where he died at age 93. At one time he held the Commission of Justice of Peace for Cumberland and in 1779 was appointed Judge of Common Pleas (Black, 1885). He is said to have been "a remarkably well proportioned man, and retained an erect and dignified bearing to old age. Black (1885) notes that: "He, at the age of 88 years, rode on horseback from Dorchester to Amherst, then thirty miles, to visit his sons residing there."

WILLIAM CHAPMAN (b c1730) and his family are listed among the passengers on the *Albion* (sailed 14 March 1774). His wife is known only as Mary (b c1732). They were married (c1754) and emigrated "on account of the rent being raised by his landlord Lord Cavendish & all necessities of life being so dear" (Tepper, 1977). Nine children are noted in the ship list. William Chapman, the pioneer, developed a prosperous farm at Point de Bute. He was a devout follower of John Wesley and deeded land for the first Methodist Church in Canada (1788).

William and Mary Chapman's fourth child, John, was 13 at the time of emigration. He married Sarah Black and settled on a large and valuable block of land in Dorchester. They raised four sons and two daughters; their second child Mary links the Chapman and the Black families with ours through her marriage to

Steeves and Colpitts Pioneers
John Weldon (b 1787).

JOHN WELDON (1732-1821) was born in Yorkshire and died in New Brunswick at the age of 89. On 20 May 1762 he married Ann Dale (1733-81) in her home town of Middleham. They settled in Crathorne Grange, in the village of Crathorne, where their four children were born (Weldon, 1953). In 1772, John Weldon sailed from London for Halifax. He was shipwrecked on the coast of Portugal. When he returned to London (1774) he found that his family had sailed from Hull on the *Albion,* 14 March 1774. He joined them in Halifax during the autumn, settled in Hillsborough in 1775 but moved to Dorchester in 1780 where he obtained land now occupied by the Penitentiary. This John Weldon (b 1732) was one of the pioneer farmers in Dorchester. His grandson John (b 1787) married Mary Chapman and settled in Coverdale. A sketch of their home is shown on page 92.. John and Mary had six children before John was drowned in the Petitcodiac River (1819) at the early age of 32 years. His widow married Enoc Stiles (1821) and they had six children.

ROBERT COLPITTS sailed on the *Jenny* 9 April 1775. His pioneering experiences in Coverdale, return to England and subsequent emigration with his family are detailed in the next chapter.

REFERENCES

Bird, W.R. 1948. When Yorkshire came to Nova Scotia. Dalhousie Review 27: 415-423.

Black, C. 1885. Historical record of the posterity of William Black. Amherst Gazette Steam Printing House, Amherst. 203 p.

Brebner, J.B. 1937. The neutral Yankees of Nova Scotia. A marginal colony during the revolutionary years. Columbia U. P., New York. 388 p.

Derry, T.K. and Jarman, T.L. 1979. Modern Britain. John Murray Publishers, London. 290 p.

Godfrey, W. 1985. Revolution rejected. Horizon Canada 2(24): 553-559.

Kerr, W.B. 1934. The rise of Michael Francklin. Dalhousie Review

13: 489-495.

Milner, W.C. 1934. History of Sackville New Brunswick. Tribune Printing Co., Sackville. 185 p.

Plumb, J.H. 1950. England in the eighteenth century. Penguin Books, Middlesex, England. 224 p.

Tepper, M. 1977. Passengers to America. Genealogical Publishing Co., Baltimore. 554 p.

Trueman, H. 1902. The Chignecto Isthmus and its first settlers. Wm. Briggs, Toronto. 268 p.

Monument marking the site of the home of Robert Colpitts and Margaret Wade Colpitts who settled on this farm in 1783, Erected November 1975 by Jean Colpitts Waddy, Seventh Generation.

94

5

THE COLPITTS PIONEERS OF NEW BRUNSWICK

An impressive granite monument marks the site of the first Colpitts homestead in Eastern Canada. Robert Colpitts, with his 'teen-age sons (John aged 15 and Robert aged 13), picked the spot on a gentle rise overlooking the intervale of the Coverdale River.[1] The spot is located about five miles up river from Salisbury; the date was 1783—probably in the late spring or early summer.

After more than two centuries, memories of this first home have long since been forgotten. Its construction must have been undertaken with some urgency since Robert's wife Margaret and five younger children were some place enroute from Halifax. From his earlier experiences of pioneering near The Bend, Robert knew something of the harsh long New Brunswick winter for which he must provide food and shelter for his large family and sufficient fuel to keep them warm and comfortable. It may already have been too late to take full advantage of the short growing season. In any case, since land must be cleared, tilled and planted, the first garden would have been a very modest one. Family tradition[2] tells only of the rigorous first year and the necessity of "living off the land."

Our pioneers left few records of the problems, frustrations, and joys of establishing a home in a remote wilderness. There were far more urgent matters than the writing of diaries; letters to the homeland were rare and few have survived. With no regular postal service, delays in transit were long and deliveries haphazard.[3] It is always fun to speculate but the fact is we know nothing of the family's first year in their new home and Robert's problems of providing for nine healthy souls. Two centuries later it is obvious that he must have planned well because the family prospered, adding two Canadian-born daughters to the seven English-born children. By the time of Robert's death in 1810, his six sons had established the Colpitts name widely throughout the expanding communities along the Little and Pollett Rivers. The Colpitts Bicentennial Reunion (1-3 July 1983) brought more than one thousand descendants back to the Salisbury and Colpitts areas. [4]

THE DECISION TO EMIGRATE

It does not take a sharp detective to conclude that Robert Colpitts and his wife Margaret dreamed of a home in Nova Scotia for many years before they secured their family roots on the Little River. They were married in the Parish church at Gainford 10 February 1768 and had three children by the time the first group of Yorkshire emigrants sailed for Halifax in 1772. At this time, the fine lands of Nova Scotia were being widely advertised in Yorkshire and neighboring Durham where most of the Colpitts family lived. The messages that were coming back to the homeland indicated that pioneering life was tolerable in spite of the "Muskatoes" and the absence of some of the finer satisfactions of life—including a Wesleyan minister. Moreover, two of Robert's first cousins (Martha Atkinson and Margaret Forster) had emigrated in 1774 [5] and their favorable reports confirmed those of other settlers. Robert, however, was evidently a cautious man and wished to see the land for himself before committing his family. As his cousin Eleanor wrote to her sister Margaret Forster in Fort Lawrence: "we are glad to embrace this favourable opertunity of sending you a letter by Cousin Robt Colpitts who is resolved of setting off to North America on Sunday first, he does not intend taking his family with him which is certainly prudent" (S. Marsh in Colpitts Bicentennial Papers, 1983).

Robert registered himself as a farmer when he signed the ship list of the *Jenny* in the spring of 1775. At this time, he and his family were evidently living near Darlington since the three younger children were born in Burtree House and christened in Haughton Le Skerne (Map p. 98). Robert was probably a small land owner or belonged to a family of land owners; he was a yeoman in the terminology of his century.[6]

Several facts indicate that the Colpitts family was prosperous and prominent in the Barnard Castle and Darlington region of Durham County: (1) Robert had the resources to undertake an exploratory trip to America; (2) he was obviously well educated for his day as evidenced by his handwriting and the phraseology in his letters and will; (3) when the family emigrated in 1783 they shipped possessions that are usually found only in more prosperous homes (for example, a well-kept family bible and three large clocks). Moreover, eighteenth century records of the lifestyles of several of the Colpitts family indicate a prominence of this name in the affairs of Durham County: there was at least one Sheriff, several agents for the Earls of Strathmore, an individual prominent enough to be buried with a slab to his memory in the church at Longbenton (near Newcastle-upon-Tyne); one person classed himself as a "Gentleman" and several belonged to fraternities of skilled workers (see E.C.Goodwin, Colpitts Bicentennial Papers, 1983). Place names associated with the fragmentary records of the Colpitts family in eighteenth century Durham are Barnard Castle, Cleatlam (about 3 miles east of Stainton, Map p. 98), Streatlam, Norton, Cockfield, Staindrop, Long Newton, Houghton Le Skerne, Winston, Swalwell, Gainford and others in the Barnard Castle region along the Tees River; the Colpitts name is still found in this part of England, particularly in and around Middlesborough.

When Robert landed in Cumberland in the spring of 1775, it is almost certain that he first delivered the letter from Eleanor Best of Barnard Castle to the Forsters at Fort Lawrence. He must have received many suggestions from his cousins of likely places to find good farming land. Whatever the advice, he evidently decided to look along the estuary of the Petitcodiac River. Ships sailing for The Bend would probably call at the ports of Dorchester and Hillsborough where other settlers might have offered further advice.

Robert selected his first land near The Bend on the south side of the Petitcodiac River. This area later became Middle Coverdale and, in the nineteenth century, Robert's site is said to have become a part of the Charles Trites farm *(The Times-Transcript,* Moncton, 23 April 1983).[7] According to family tradition, he clear-

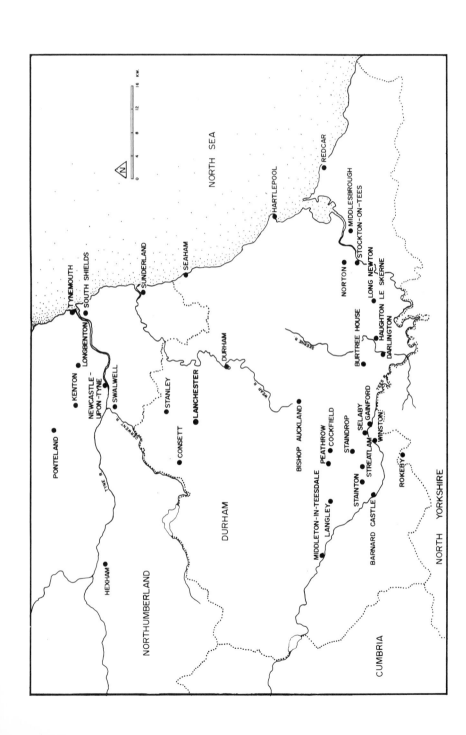

ed some land, built a small cabin, planted and harvested his first crop; he then spent the winter of '75-'76 in Canada and planted another crop in the spring of 1776 before returning to England expecting to bring his family to Nova Scotia before harvest time. Robert *may have* "started from scratch" as tradition has it, but speculation should be tempered with knowledge of the early Acadian activities on the south shore of the Petitcodiac. The maps of 1755 and 1786 (pp. 2 and 104) show many Acadian homes between Le Coude (now Moncton) and Rivière aux Crapauds (now Turtle Creek). Major Scott's expedition of 1758 concentrated primarily on the north shore of the river; it was many years before the last of the Acadians moved from the south shore to the Fox Creek, Dover or Memramcook areas. Robert may well have started in an abandoned Acadian home with an established kitchen garden and some cleared land. The fact is we have no details whatever of Robert's life during his first year in Nova Scotia but we can be certain that he did not find the desolate and unoccupied country that some of his descendants have imagined.

THE YEARS OF WAITING

There are no certain records relevant to Robert's return to Durham County or the family fortunes during the six years that they waited and dreamed of life on the Petitcodiac River. History suggests a chronology: The Declaration of Independence was signed on 4 July 1776 and, during the same year Tory refugees were arriving in Halifax from Boston and the word "Loyalist" was acquiring a new meaning in the English language; also in '76, raiding parties of New Englanders were creating havoc along the Bay of Fundy and the lower Petitcodiac estuary (Wright, 1945). Even though news travelled very slowly two centuries ago, Robert must

---

Map of Durham County, England based on Ordnance Survey Maps. 1:50,000. Sheets 88, 92, 93 (1979). Published by Director of Ordnance Survey Southampton, England.

have realized that it was time to return to his family. The problem of finding ship passage would have been a very real one; he might have sailed from The Bend to Saint John [8] in the hope of finding a vessel bound for England but this is unlikely with Halifax the bustling center of maritime activity during the war. He probably visited the cousins at Fort Lawrence and might have sailed from Cumberland but the Bay was infested with privateers and New England raiders. Halifax was the logical port and it is unlikely that Robert lingered there any longer than absolutely necessary. Of Halifax in 1776, Raddall (p. 91, 1971) writes:

> . . . the town bustled with English and Scotch soldiers in red, Germans in blue, and Nova Scotians in green, with prisoners, French and American, in rags of all hues, with refugee loyalists of every grade from rich to destitute, with oddly dressed negro slaves, with tough and reckless privateersmen, with solemn "Dutch" market gardeners hawking their wares, with larking jack-tars and bullying press gangs . . .

When did Robert Colpitts reach his homeland? The fact that son Ralph was born in January 1778 suggests a home coming late in 1776 or early in 1777. According to family tradition, he promptly settled his affairs and headed for Newcastle-upon-Tyne anticipating a quick end of hostilities and an early departure for Canada. However, the war dragged on and by this time the American Revolution had taken on much broader dimensions; France aligned herself with the rebels and declared war against Britain early in 1778; with the French fleet prowling the Atlantic and both Holland and Spain in sympathy with the American cause, a move to Nova Scotia was impossible.

Speculation concerning a move to Newcastle should be cautious because Ralph was born at Peathrow early in 1778 and christened at Cockfield—both located in County Durham about nine miles north-east of Barnard Castle (Map p. 98). The only certain record of the family in Northumberland is the birth of George (1782) in Kenton with a christening in Ponteland, both places located in the environs of Newcastle-upon-Tyne. By 1782 the Revolutionary War had come to an end and emigration must then have seemed feasible; although the Peace of Paris was not signed until 1783, the fighting really ended with the decisive battles of 1781.

Our New Brunswick Colpitts relatives believe that their ancestors

100

operated a toll bridge while they waited in Newcastle-upon-Tyne. This tradition is so firmly held that it seems entirely likely although the commitment may have been much shorter than the traditional "seven long years." The control of a toll gate in eighteenth century England was a far more significant responsibility than the experiences of our century might suggest. These were the days when a good network of passable roads, bridges and canals was being developed, and toll gates had become an important part of life and travel. There are many records of the deplorable travel conditions in earlier times when many of the roads were little more than bridle-paths, unfit for any kind of wheeled vehicle. During the earlier years of the century, an agricultural expert advised travellers to avoid the roads around Newcastle "which must either dislocate their bones or bury them in muddy sand." Other roads were described as "ponds of liquid dirt. . . so narrow that a mouse cannot pass any carriage." See Darry and Jarman (1979).

The eighteenth century solution to road problems was the Turnpike Trusts. These came into existence gradually during the early part of the century—largely through the requirements of the army. A Trust consisted of local people who invested in the improvement and maintenance of a stretch of road and then recovered their expenditures by operating a toll gate. The Trusts were recognized by law in 1773 and toll gates became almost universal; in the years that followed, some of the great road builders of history began to produce smooth and durable road surfaces—John Loudon MacAdam, a Scotsman, for example. Tolls varied with the type of vehicle (coach, carriage, horse- or donkey-rider), and consequently the toll keeper was in a position of authority and responsibilities that must have required tact and intelligence. How long the Colpitts family may have been engaged in this activity or where they were located is still a mystery.

THE MOVE TO NOVA SCOTIA [9]

At about the time Robert and Margaret's youngest son George was born (12 September 1782), some 600 Loyalists were gathering together their possessions and boarding ships in New York bound for Annapolis, Nova Scotia (Wright, 1955). This news would have reached the Colpitts family during the autumn of 1782 with disturbing rumors that much larger numbers of loyalist emigrants would be transported to Nova Scotia during the following spring. This obviously meant that the best lands would become more and more difficult to obtain. Actually, the deciding battles of the Revolution were fought in 1781 and it would have been well known in England that the terms of peace were being negotiated in Paris and that the colonies would probably be given their independence and that large numbers of Loyalists would be encouraged or forced to move. In the end, some 35,000 were transported or found their way to Nova Scotia which, at that time, included New Brunswick. The Colpitts family must have spent an anxious winter speculating on their chances of finding good land and impatient to emigrate just as soon as possible.

Someone may yet find a ship list, a long-lost letter or an old diary that will establish the details of the Colpitts' departure for Canada. In spite of many hours of searching, the date of departure, the name of the ship and its time of arrival are unknown. It is assumed that they sailed from Newcastle-upon-Tyne in the spring of 1783 and arrived in Halifax some weeks later. There is no account of their journey; it was probably similar to that of many other passages of sailing ships at that time. Charles Dixon, one of the first of the Yorkshire immigrants who sailed on the *Duke of York* 16 March 1772 with 62 emigrants wrote that:

> We had a rough passage. None of us having been to sea before, much sea-sickness prevailed. At Halifax we were received with much joy by the gentlemen in general, but were much discouraged by others, and the account given us of Cumberland was enough to make the stoutest give way (Trueman, 1902).

Ten years would have changed opinions of Cumberland and it must have seemed a most desirable goal in comparison with their landing port, Halifax. To quote Raddall once more:

> In 1783 the war ended at last; and with the evacuation of New York, the last royal stronghold, came the final hegira of the loyalists. By November more than twenty-five thousand

refugees were in Nova Scotia, half of whom landed in Halifax. On their heels came a great part of the British army. "Every shed, outhouse, store and shelter was crowded with people. Thousands were under canvas on the Citadel and . . . indeed everywhere that tents could be pitched. . . . Cabooses and cookhouses were brought ashore from the ships and the people were fed near them on Granville and Hollis streets. There were many deaths and all the miseries and unsanitary conditions of an overcrowded town. For four months the bulk of ten thousand refugees were fed on the streets, amongst them many reared and nurtured in every comfort in the homes they had to fly from. . . . In contrast with this vast misery, and cheek by jowl with it, flourished the gay life of the army and navy officers, with wealthier loyalists, the prosperous contractors, shipowners and others who had made money out of the war. The town swarmed with discharged soldiers and sailors dissolute in the sudden letdown after eight years of war. . . . "the people in general are almost as dark and vile as Sodom." [Raddall, pp. 95-96, 1971].

Halifax was certainly no place for a family of staunch Methodists. Perhaps the cousins from Fort Lawrence met the Colpitts family and helped them sort out their lives in the new world. There are no records. Family tradition tells that Robert with the two eldest sons started overland to his long-dreamed-of plot of land in Coverdale while Margaret and the five other children with the family belongings trans-shipped for Cumberland at the head of the Bay of Fundy.

In 1783, Robert and his sons had an option of two primitive roads leading north from Halifax, one going to Truro and the other (somewhat shorter) to Windsor. Overland travel beyond either of these points was unlikely since there were no roads but there were well-travelled water routes leading to Shepody Bay and on up the Petitcodiac estuary. Vessels bound for The Bend probably docked at Hopewell Cape, Dorchester and Hillsborough where Robert may have contacted Yorkshire settlers, some of whom travelled with him on the *Jenny* in 1775; they would have had many stories to tell of changes on the upper Petitcodiac. By 1783 Christian and Frederick Stief were established on the Stief lands eight miles west of The Bend and their brothers in Hillsborough were probably well informed on conditions along

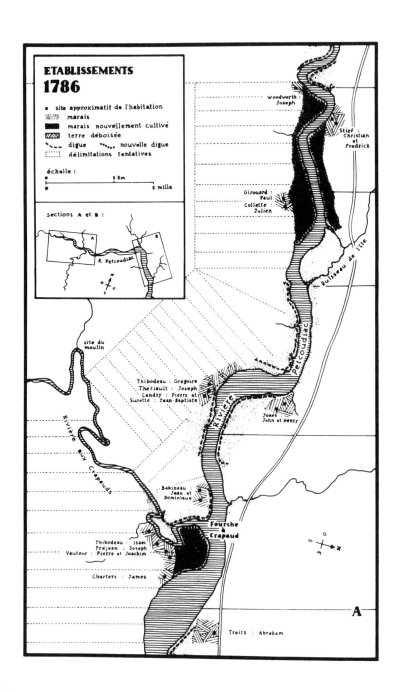

ETABLISSEMENTS
1786

- • site approximatif de l'habitation
- marais
- marais nouvellement cultivé
- terre déboisée
- digue   nouvelle digue
- délimitations tentatives

échelle :

1 Km

1 mille

sections A et B :

R. Petcoudiac

site du
moulin

Thibodeau : Grégoire
Thériault : Joseph
Landry : Pierre et
Surette : Jean-Baptiste

Jonet
John et Henry

Babineau
Jean et
Dominique

Fourche
à
Crapaud

Thibodeau : Isaac
Préjean : Joseph
Vautour : Pierre et Joachim

Charters : James

Treitz : Abraham

Woodworth
Joseph

Stief :
Christian
et
Fredrick

Girouard :
Paul
Collette :
Julien

Ruisseau de l'île

Petcoudiac

Rivière

Rivière aux Crapauds

A

the Petitcodiac. Long before Robert reached the Coverdale area he must have realized that "his plot of land" had been taken over by others. The map of 1786 shows several groups of Acadian homes along the south shore of the Petitcodiac and two establish-ed newcomers—James Charters [10] whose farmlands appear to be located close to the area where Robert settled in 1775 and Joseph Woodworth farther up river in the Boundary Creek area; both were from New England (Wright, 1982).

Robert and his sons decided to look for land in the Salisbury area where Yorkshire people were already living. For example, Joshua Geldart who emigrated on the *Albion* in 1774 bought 583 acres of land from George Wortman in 1778 and was probably well established in Salisbury by 1783. The Colpitts men are said to have searched around Salisbury but, not finding land that ap-peared suitable, continued their explorations along the Little River a major branch of the Petitcodiac. They were not the first to explore this lovely tributary; Ganong (1930) notes Acadian homes 1.5 miles south of Salisbury on the Little River. Apparently Major Scott's expedition of 1758 missed them or did not consider a search along the tributaries of the Petitcodiac to be worthwhile.

About five miles from Salisbury, Robert and his sons decided to locate on a lovely piece of intervale with nearby stands of sugar maple. Perhaps the spot reminded him of his native land; to me the Little River at this point is not unlike the River Tees in the Barnard Castle area of Durham County, England. In any case, their selection proved to be a wise one for these lands have now been productively farmed for more than two centuries and are still in the hands of Colpitts descendants.

There are no records of Margaret's journey from Halifax with the five younger children. She may have visited with the cousins

---

Locations of homes along the Petitcodiac River, west of The Bend in 1786. Light stipple, marshland; heavy stipple, newly cultivated marshland. Reproduced from "Le Grand Petcoudiac." Volume III of "Histoire des Trois-Rivières" by Paul Surette (1985). Maps by author; graphics by Bernard LeBlanc. Courtesy of Paul Surette.

in Fort Lawrence until Robert had a home ready. Tradition has it that they were united during the summer of 1783 but that it was too late to plant a crop and the following winter was most difficult and monotonous with a diet that emphasized salmon and game. The first certain records of life in Canada are the births of two daughters—Margaret born 11 October 1784 and Jane born 3 October 1786. Their mother died in 1794 and was buried in a plot of farmland not far from her Canadian home. [11]

ROBERT'S LATER YEARS

Within one year, the Colpitts family that emigrated to Nova Scotia in 1783, found themselves living in a new colony called New Brunswick. Many factors led to the partition of the old colony but the strong pressures and skilled negotiations of the Loyalists in Parrtown [12] dominated all of them   (Wright, pp. 124-150, 1955; MacNutt, pp. 95-102, 1965; Wynn, 1985). The division was formally ordered in London on 18 June 1784 and, in November of the same year, the government of New Brunswick was proclaimed in Parrtown. Actually, these political changes had very little effect on the pioneers of south-eastern New Brunswick. The thousands of Loyalists that settled at the mouth of the St. John River and in its peaceful valley put a completely new stamp on the western regions of the colony while, by contrast, only a handfull of Loyalists located along the Petitcodiac where settlement was left to the pre-loyalist New Englanders, the Pennsylvania Dutch, the Yorkshire people and other waves of Europeans that followed them.

On 25 November 1784, the new Governor Thomas Carleton

Intervale of the Little River where Robert Colpitts settled in 1783, as seen today. Family burial plot immediately right of bridge; home site where monument is now located, near skeleton of elm tree about 5 cm from right margin of picture. The Bamford Colpitts Bridge was built elsewhere and moved to this site in the 1930s.

issued a Proclamation requiring all persons who held land under the government of Nova Scotia to register their lands within a certain time limit. New land grants were to be based on family size and Robert and his six sons did well, acquiring several thousand acres in their new homeland. Maps of the original land grants in Colpitts Settlement show a major block of 1000 acres in the names of Robert and George Colpitts jointly, and directly south of this a parcel of 300 acres granted to Margaret Colpitts and one of equal size to the eldest son John. The name Colpitts appears on several smaller blocks of land in this area so that in all the Colpitts family held over 2,000 acres in what became known as Colpitts Settlement (Grant Index Plan No. 131. Dep't Natur. Resources and Energy, Crown Lands Branch, Fredericton, N.B.). The same map shows original land grants along the Pollett River, a major branch of the Petitcodiac to the west and parallel to the Little River. Around the turn of the century, the three sons William, Thomas and Ralph acquired grants totalling over 2,000 acres along the Pollett between The Glades and the village of Pollett River (Map p. 8). They were among the pioneers of this area but not the first to settle there; Christopher Horsman, Jr., who married their youngest sister Jane is said to have been the first (Pincombe, 1969).[13]

Scattered records show that the first Robert Colpitts to arrive in Canada played his part in the affairs of the emerging province of New Brunswick. In 1786 his name appears among twelve others on a petition to the Governor, Council and House of Assembly of the province requesting the opening of a road from "Petcoodiack to the city of St. John," and also for the escheat of lands left vacant by absentee landlords. At this time, there were still blocks of fine land assigned to distant landlords who had done nothing to discharge the terms of their agreements. The absentee owners —in the words of the petition—were "a Publick Nuisance to the Settlements" and "we further beg that no further land be granted but to such as occupy the area" (see Elizabeth Goodwin, 1981, in the Colpitts Bicentennial Papers, 1983). Another record concerns Robert's military service as Captain in the New Brunswick Militia. He joined the Westmorland County Regiment on 21 April 1806 and served until his death; son Ralph is listed as an Ensign in the same unit.[14]

Facey-Crowther (1984) traces the history of the New Brunswick

Militia which had its origins in the provincial militia act of 1787. From the time of the French Wars (1793) through the war of 1812-14, the militia met with public approval but after about 1830 support declined except for short flurries of activity during real or perceived crises such as the Aroostook War (1839) or the Fenian Raids of 1866[15] and during the occasional royal visits. The unit was disbanded after Confederation when in 1868 the Dominion passed its first Militia Act.

After Margaret's death in 1794, Robert remarried. His second wife is known only by the name "Elizabeth;" the official record of the marriage has not been found. Jean Colpitts Waddy (personal communication) believes that Elizabeth was the widow of John Newton (Fort Lawrence) who died in 1807. John Newton's will is dated 9 February 1797[16] when according to the text of the will, he was "Sick and weak in body, but of perfect mind and Memory . . . calling unto mind the Mortallity of my body, and knowling that [it] is appointed unto all Men once to die . . . " Then, following the usual provisions for "Christian Burial" his bequests were "First, I give and bequeath to my beloved Sister Ann & her Son John the Sum of five pounds currency. . . . Also I give to my dearly beloved Wife Elizabeth Newton, whome I likewise constitute, make and ordain the Sole Executrix of this my last Will and Testament, all and Singular my lands, Messuages, goods and Chattles by her freely to be possessed and enjoyed, and to be at her only will and disposal."

If Robert's second wife was Elizabeth Newton, it is evident that they did not enjoy life together for many years. Robert died in 1810 at the age of 65—relatively young by today's standards when many are looking forward to the less hectic years of retirement. Two letters among the family papers indicate that a painful medical problem took some of the joy out of his last years. The diagnosis of the time was "the gravel" but from the symptoms described in these letters, he might equally well have been suffering from an enlarged prostate. Whatever the problem, he evidently suffered great agony in an age before ultrasound shattered kidney stones or skilled surgeons relieved the problems of a blocked urethra. I quote some passages from photocopies of these letters supplied by Jean Waddy. The first, dated 6 April 1809 is from John Fawcet of Sackville addressed to Mrs. Elizabeth Colpitts, Hillsborough.

Dear Sister in the Lord

I Sit down, to write you a few lines, to acquaint you with the situation of your Dear Husband, who arrived at our House last Evening, about Eight O Clock, very poorly in Body, being seized with the Gravel, he was taken in the afternoon, & it was with dificulty he reached our House, where he has been mostly confined to his Bed since he came, he has had the Doctor this Evning, who has given him much relief, he is a good deel easyer in Body, and quite Comfortable in his mind, and much resigned to the will of the Lord. . . . I hope you will endeaviur to look up to the Lord and Stay your Self upon god, under whose present Dispensation of Providence, your Dear Husband is in the hands of a gratious god, who is two wise to err, and two merciful to be rigorous with his creatures . . .

Two days later Robert made his will. It was witnessed by A. Botsford, John Fawcet who wrote the above letter and Timothy Richardson who is mentioned in his letter of 10 April when he wrote to "My Dear Betty" and was able to assure her that "I have settled my worldly affairs and am resigned to my Heavenly Father's will . . . Excerpts from this letter written four days after his seizure follow:

I got very well down to Timothy Richardson on Tuesday Evening and was well on Wednesday till after noon. I had no Sickness but I could not make Water after that I set out for John Fawcets and with much Difficulty got there between Eight and Nine in the Evening . . . all very much alarmed my pain encreased all Night and next Day . . . Thursday afternoon I sent . . . Doctor Smith. he came that Evening let me Blood gave me some Meddicines and about an hour after let off my water by means of Silver pipe for that purpose. after that I went to Sleep and only waked once during the Night and free from all pain and uneasiness the Doctor staid all Night and gave me a dose of Salts in the Morning which worked very well, I have been tollerably Easy ever since but I have made no Water yet without using the Instrument as above. I can use it my self and do not find it painfull in the opperation and when the water is discharged

I am quite at ease and can Sleep and Eat as well as I could wish to do I keep mostly to my bed but it is more to keep from cold, than by reason of sickness . . . my Dear Betty I beg you will not make your self uneasy for my sittuation, but . . . It hath Pleased Almighty God to afflict my body and I may yet be Sanctified for the good of my Soul. I find my mind very happy and can see how gracious the Lord is to such an unworthy creature as me in Laying his Correcting hand upon me in this Place where I can have the use of means being used for the relief of my Mortal Body. I have been visited by a number of Christian friends . . . and prayed very devoutly with me and for me . . .

Blessing of God Rest upon you and all my Family and Neighbours and may you and they be all happy to Eternity I am Dear Betty

your Loving Husband

Robert Colpitts

A copy of Robert's last will and testament, dated 8 April 1809, is included as Appendix A. The penmanship differs from that of the above letter; perhaps one of his friends or the lawyer wrote the will for him. The text of the will affirms his strong sense of justice and his abiding religious faith. The phraseology of his letter as well as the will show that he was well educated for his day—as were many of the Yorkshire immigrants. Robert Colpitts died in 1810, a year after the letters were written describing his medical problems so graphically.

The progenitors of the New Brunswick Colpitts family lie buried in a small plot of ground not far from the first Colpitts home.[1] If their ghosts roam the area, they must be well pleased. Today, the lands that Robert and his two eldest sons selected in 1783 remain productively farmed by seventh generation descendants. Robert and Margaret's children and grandchildren opened up several communities in south-eastern New Brunswick and the family name is now found throughout Canada and in many places in the United States.

THE SECOND AND THIRD GENERATIONS

This book deals primarily with my mother's lineage (Chart p. 130). If Robert Colpitts, the progenitor of the New Brunswick family, is considered first generation Canadian, then his son Ralph (my great-great-grandfather) was second generation even though he was born in Peathrow, England about nine miles from Barnard Castle in Durham County. Ralph was born on New Year's day 1778—the first child following Robert's return from his Canadian adventure in 1775. He was a lad of about eight when the family arrived in the Little River country. Like his five brothers and three sisters, he grew up under very primitive pioneer conditions. There were no public schools in New Brunswick at that time and Ralph, like the other small children, must have learned the three Rs from their well-educated parents.[17] Many of our ancestors in this generation grew up illiterate and "made their mark" on official documents. This was not true of Robert's family; Ralph's signature survives as does a letter that he wrote to his brother Robert following the death of his first wife.

Ralph's first wife was Maria (Miriam) Jones of Moncton. Her ancestors [18] were among the Pennsylvania Dutch immigrants who landed at the mouth of Hall's Creek in 1766. When most of the Pennsylvania immigrants moved to Hillsborough, Charles Jones with his family, as well as the Trites family remained on their lands in Monckton Township. Charles Jones' lands were immediately to the east of those of Heinrich Stief (Map p. 43) and when the land grants were sorted out and confirmed in later years, his sons John and Henry jointly received almost 2,500 acres located between the Frederick Stief holdings to the west and those of Charles Baker (later James Charters) to the east.

When Robert homesteaded in Coverdale in 1775-76, the Jones family would have been near neighbors, within easy reach by boat across the Petitcodiac River at high tide. In all probability Robert renewed his acquaintances with the Jones family when he journeyed up river to Salisbury in 1783; there could have been many contacts over the years before the families were joined in the marriage of Ralph and Maria 16 January 1806. During the next seventeen years, Robert and Maria added 10 grandchildren to the rapidly expanding flock of our progenitors Robert and Margaret. The last two seem to have been twins (daughters) and their mother died at the time of their birth.[19]

Only scraps of information concerning Ralph the man remain after more than a century and a half. However, that is more than one can say about many of the eighteenth century ancestors. In total, my conclusion is that this great-great-grandfather was an exceedingly pious man, a loving husband, a dedicated father, a good provider, and a concerned citizen. His moral philosophy (and sense of poetry) are obvious in the letter that he wrote 20 December 1823 to his brother Robert living in Sussex Vale. The first two and the last two paragraphs are included here; the complete text may be found in the Colpitts Bicentennial Papers (1983):

Dear Brother

I take my pen with a sorrowful heart to inform you that God in his wise providence has seen fit to take from me my beloved partner in life and left me to mourn my loss. I feel like one alone in the wilderness, the world with its busy scenes has now no delight to afford me and society has lost its pleasure as I have not my Maria to share it with me. My house seems empty and the very doors on their hinges speaks her loss.

When I look upon my dear little children who are now bereaved of a kind parent, how shall I describe my feelings, they have no fond Mother to listen to their prattle or make their complaints unto, her careful hand no longer feeds them nor calls their vivacity to order, no she is gone to return no more to us.

. . .

113

Thus my dear Brother I have tried to give you some faint ideas of my trouble, I know that you will sympathize with me, but you cannot relieve me, if you can pray for me, pray, that my afflictions may be sanctified, and that my hopes may be more than made up in the enjoyments of those felicities which I trust my Maria is now in full possession of.

With respect to the little Infants, the one is with my Sister Horsman and the other with Sister Eunice, my best respects to Sister Rachel and all the family. I remain with all due affection

Dear Brother yours

Ralph Colpitts

Ralph's prowess as a hunter is mentioned in all the family papers. Hunting and fishing were basic to survival (and health) in pioneering Canada. Wild game was abundant in the New Brunswick wilderness and rivers like the Pollett teamed with salmon and trout. His hunting abilities must have been exceptional to be the subject of comment in an age when hunting and fishing were a part of life.

The last note that I have to offer on great-great-grandfather Ralph relates to his military service. He joined the Westmorland Regiment of the New Brunswick Militia on 21 April 1806. He is listed as an Ensign in the First Battalion where his father was a Captain. I have no record of the length of service; he died in 1856 at a time when the unit had almost ceased to exist except on paper (Facey-Crowther, 1984).

THE VALE CALLED PLEASANT

Go to the Valley named Pleasant!
Its charms you will quickly behold.
Go to the Valley named Pleasant!
Its beauty shall never grow old.

A century has passed since the valley
Was chosen for man's abode.
The forefathers named it wisely,
For "Pleasant" was the name bestowed.

Celia M. Colpitts Bishop [20]

Ralph Colpitts (b 1778) fathered five sons followed by six daughters. In the early 1830s, when it was time for the sons to leave the family nest, the older boys elected to establish homes and develop farms on the Little River about 15 miles south of Colpitts Settlement. Here they obtained grants totalling 1000 acres or more in the area that became known as Pleasant Vale. All five sons seem to have had original land grants (Grant Index Plan No. 131, Crown Lands Branch, Fredericton, N.B.) but when matters were finally sorted out Robert, Thomas and Charles became the pioneer farmers "in the vale" while Ralph (son of Ralph b 1778) remained on the family farm; [21] at an early stage in the history of Pleasant Vale, Henry the eldest son was killed by a falling tree.[22]

To appreciate the flavor and comfort of life in the third generation of Colpitts pioneers, drive to the cross-roads in Pleasant Vale where a highway running west to Mapleton and Elgin about seven miles distant is crossed by one running north-south. A small white church without steeple (once Methodist now United) [23] stands in one angle of the cross with Robert's old home across the north-south road on the hillside opposite; the Thomas Colpitts home where my grandmother was born is located diagonally across from Robert's and the rural school occupied the fourth angle of the cross. These two beautiful homes still stand after more than a century and a half. The original Charles Colpitts farm was located next to the Thomas Colpitts farm on the road leading south; this home still exists also.

MEMORY'S PICTURES

As a child, I sensed my mother's satisfaction at the prospect of a family jaunt to Pleasant Vale. Trips of this distance (about 30 miles) were not frequent. Farm life with its unending chores and the demands of the farm animals do not leave time for holidays. Besides, dad's ties were on the opposite side of Albert County, down Hopewell Hill way, where a visit to the ageing grandmother, aunts, uncles and cousins was a rare treat. But there were occasional trips to Pleasant Vale and these became more frequent after 1921 when the first family car made possible a one-day jaunt of 30 miles.

A few scattered memories remain after almost three-quarters of a century: the gently rounded and lush hillsides with sheep and frolicking lambs in springtime, large homes (always white in my memories), similar to the one shown on the opposite page, with nearby barns, out buildings, gardens, orchards and shade trees. The atmosphere in these homes was warm with loving relatives, cosy wood stoves, and tantalizing aromas of home cooking; everything was neat and tidy and everyone seemed to know what was expected of them. It seemed a very comfortable life style.

Autumn and spring trips were particularly memorable because of the great stands of sugar maple (*Acer saccharinum* Linn.) with their gorgeous autumn colors and their inviting sugar camps in the spring. A trip to a sugar bush was a rare and exciting adventure. Several of the second and third generation ancestors were pioneers in sugar making along the Pollett and Little Rivers. In the 1840s, according to Maimie Steeves (p. 73):

> . . . the first sugar-making enterprise of the country was started. Robert Colpitts is said to have tried it out on a small scale first, then formed a small local industry with William Colpitts . . . along the Pollett River . . . and with Christian and Abel Steeves of Coverdale along the Little River. During the first season . . . they made 6,200 pounds of sugar. It was no easy task, containers called "cassas" were made by hand of bark from the white birch; "spiles" made of small branches with the pitch removed or "truffets" made of hollowed out chips were driven into the bark below the holes made for the sap to flow out; the sweet drip was exasperatingly slow, increased by bright sunshine following a frosty night. The cassas were emptied into wooden buckets, usually

---

Pioneer home of Thomas Colpitts and Ann Margaret (Weldon) Colpitts built about 1838 in Pleasant Vale, Albert County. In succeeding generations of the Colpitts family, this home was occupied by John Arthur McNutt Colpitts (Captain Arthur), George Colpitts and Curtis Colpitts. It is now owned by Charles E. Barbour.

M. LABADIE 1988

Sugar Camp Operated by Everett Steeves 1988
Between Pleasant Vale and Elgin

carried on a neck yoke, and the liquid carried to the huge fire where it was boiled down in large iron cauldrons. The fire was never allowed to go out while the sugar season lasted, so that no small part of the business was the supplying of fuel. Once the sugar was made, it had to be hauled to the river, a task in itself when hillsides were soggy and slippery with March snows. This was also done by hand, the sugar piled high on a toboggan. At the river it was loaded into canoes—pine dug-outs, the only kind on the Pollett and Petitcodiac in those days—and taken to the "Bend" or exchanged with any settlers along the bank who were lucky enough to have goods for trading purposes.

Our ancestors learned the art of harvesting maple sugar from the Acadians who, in turn, had learned it from the Micmacs. The first account of sugar making appears in the Publications of the Royal Society of London in 1685. In an abridged form it reads: [24]

The savages of Canada, in the season when the sap rises in the maple, make an incision in the tree, by which it runs out; and after they have evaporated 8 pounds of the liquor, there remains 1 pound, as sweet and as much sugar, as that which is got out of canes; part of the same sugar is sent to be refined in Rouen. The savages have practised this art longer than any, now living among them, can remember.

Before the Micmacs obtained iron pots from Europeans, the sap was evaporated by putting red-hot stones into wooden dug-out troughs filled with sap; the Indians also knew that some water could be removed by freezing and removing the ice. Maple sugar was used extensively by the native people and was the only source of sugar for the first Acadians; during the 1800s, cane sugar gradually replaced the maple product. At first, the two were blended but as the cane became less and less expensive and more readily available, the maple product ceased to be used for general purposes.

There have been many advances in techniques since our ancestors established the first New Brunswick sugar industry. Sap is still collected by traditional methods of "tapping" the trees by drilling a hole in the trunk and inserting a faucet (spile and spout) which allows the sap to drip into large metal pails; the sap is periodically collected and boiled in great evaporator tanks with clouds of steam rising into the springtime air until the liquid becomes concentrated to the maple syrup stage; [25] if sugar is desired, further concentration is carried out in large iron cauldrons. However, many large operators now use miles of plastic tubing to carry the sap from the trees and, in some operations, vacuum pumps draw the sap from the trees to the sugar camp; large volumes of water may also be removed by reverse osmosis rather than the labor intensive operations of stoking great wood fires and operating evaporation tanks. Maple products are now a luxury item and not the important part of the diet that they were in Micmac and Acadian times. [26]

The relatives that we visited in the Vale are gone now.[27] The three Colpitts ancestors of the third generation who pioneered this pleasant valley, raised large families and settled their sons on nearby farms—typically with one exception who went elsewhere for a professional education. The Colpitts name—so common here for most of a century—is now found only on their grave stones on the hillside. A prosperous farming community for more than a century, Pleasant Vale like many other New Brunswick farming areas, has moved into another century. The forests are gradually creeping over many of the hills and dales, while the lovely old homes have been modernized to become country residences or bedrooms for city workers. It seems fitting to close this chapter with a few verses of Celia Colpitts Bishop's "Pioneer Days and Now."

> We had a glimpse of Pioneer Days
>   When we were children small;
> And clearly I remember
>   The spinning wheel by the wall.
>
>   . . .
>
> Yes times have changed since then.
>   Oxen, no longer teamed,
> And tractors do the heavy work
>   Which only for them seemed.

120

The speeding horse is out of style.
Rough roads are going too.
And now the motor cars spin by
On pavements wide and new.

Factories are making all the soap,
And dyes of every hue.
The mills are making yards of cloth
Which Mother used to do.

. . .

Candles are used for ornament
Oil lamps are seldom lit.
Electric lights now shine about
Where'er we walk and sit.

. . .

This is an age of ease and speed
Compared with the pioneer.
But did they have more happiness
Whose hearts were full of cheer?

REFERENCES

Bishop, C.M.C. c1955. Memories in rhymes down in the Maritimes. L'Imprimerie Acadienne Ltee. 82 p.

Campbell, G.G. 1948. A history of Nova Scotia. Ryerson, Toronto. 288 p.

Colpitts Bicentennial Papers. 1983. File in Province of New Brunswick Archives (Fredericton) includes a special paper on the Colpitts Family by Elizabeth Colpitts Goodwin (1981, 11 p.) and five Newsletters issued during the planning of the Bicentennial of 1983.

Colpitts, G.A. 1963. Pioneers of New Brunswick. The "John Branch" of the Colpitts family. Author Publication, Carberry, Manitoba. 133 p.

Derry, T.K. and Jarman, T.L. 1979. Modern Britain. John Murray, London. 390 p.

Facey-Crowther, D.R. 1984. The New Brunswick Militia. Commissioned officers' list 1787-1867. N.B. Genealog. Soc. Fredericton, N.B. *Also* The New Brunswick Militia: 1784-1871. Master's Thesis by Facey-Crowther. Univ. N.B. Library, Fredericton.

Ganong, W.F. 1930. The report and map of Major Scott's expedition to remove the French from the Petitcodiac in 1758. Coll. N.B. Hist. Soc. 13: 97-114.

Graves, D.E. 1986. For Ireland. Horizon Canada 5(49): 1153-1159.

Larracey, E.W. 1970. The first hundred. Moncton Pub. Co., Moncton. 306 p.

Lanken, D. 1987. We're killing our maples. Can. Geogr. 107(1): 16-27.

MacNutt, W.S. 1965. The Atlantic Provinces. McClelland & Stewart, Toronto. 305 p.

MacPhee, E.D. (ed.) The story of R.R.Colpitts & Son 1902-1962. 60 years in Moncton, N.B. (no date, no publisher). 51 p.

Pincombe, C.A. 1969. The history of Monckton Township (CA. 1700-1875). Thesis Univ. N.B. [Microfilm No. 5694. NL-101 (1/66). Nat. Library of Canada, Ottawa.] 339 p.

Raddall, T.H. 1971. Halifax. Warden of the North (revised). McClelland & Stewart, Toronto. 343 p.

Ross, E. 1986. Post haste. Horizon Canada. 6(66): 1568-1573.

Schapiro, J.S. and Morris R.B. 1938. Civilization in Europe and the world. Copp Clark, Toronto. 809 p.

Steeves, Maimie [Wilbur] No date. Fundy folklore. Albert County Hist. Soc. 106 p. [A series of Moncton Newspaper articles written in the 1940s].

Taylor, R.M. and Crandall, R.J. (eds). 1986. Generations and change. Mercer Univ. Press, Macon, Georgia. 332 p.

Thompson, J. 1987. Drawing the line. Horizon Canada 9(100): 2384-2389.

Trueman, H. 1902. The Chignecto Isthmus and its first settlers. Wm Briggs, Toronto. 268 p.

Wright, E.C. 1945. The Petitcodiac. Tribune Press, Sackville. 76 p.

Wright, E.C. 1955. The loyalists of New Brunswick. Lancelot Press, Hantsport. 364 p. [Available from Author].

Wright, E.C. 1982. Planters and pioneers (revised). Lancelot Press, Hantsport. 334 p. [Available from Author].

Wynn, G. 1985. Paradise north. Horizon Canada 3(33): 769-775.

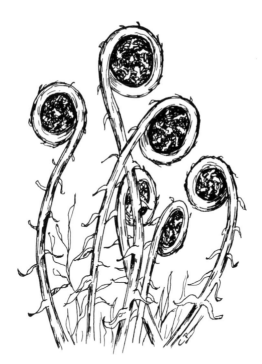

Fiddleheads
While relatives along the estuary of the Petitcodiac feasted on marsh greens, the ancestors on the Little and Pollett Rivers dined on fiddleheads, the springtime shoots of the Ostrich Fern. Sketch by Carole Parlee. x0.75.

6

ANCESTRY OF AMANDA ANGELINE COLPITTS

This chapter includes biographical notes on Amanda Colpitts' direct ancestors with a catalogue of her forbears and near relatives. The lists of relatives are incomplete since only the "John Branch" of the Colpitts family has been researched and published in detail (G.A.Colpitts, 1962). Although many of Clayton D. Colpitts' records are sketchy, his *The Colpitts from Yorkshire* (1956) was a most useful source for my lists of family members. Data for the second generation were compiled by Jean Colpitts Waddy who obtained many records from the late Harold Colpitts and others from Sterling Marsh and Anna Chavelle. Some families are listed in Weldon (1953) and Wright (1965); I have tried to cross-check these. Although the lists remain incomplete, they may form a basis for future genealogists interested in the Colpitts family.

ROBERT COLPITTS--FIRST GENERATION CANADIAN

(1) ROBERT COLPITTS	M	MARGARET WADE
1745-1810	1768	1747-94

Robert and Margaret were married in the parish church at Gainford on 10 February 1768. Robert's bride belonged to a prosperous family; in the words of one who has studied the *Wade Papers* (Public Archives of Canada, Ottawa) "a farming family with considerable capital, and . . . strict Methodists." Robert's ancestry in England is still incompletely documented. Present evidence indi-

124

cates that he was born 27 June 1745 at Winston, the son of John Colpitts of Selaby (b 1696) and Elizabeth Jackson who were married at Winston 14 February 1727. [1] John of Selaby was the son of Thomas Colpitts of Barfort and Mary Barnes of Cleatlam, married 14 November 1688.[2] Thus, Thomas Colpitts and Mary Barnes would have been the grandparents of Robert, our progenitor. [3]

The Family of Robert Colpitts and Margaret Wade

JOHN (1768-94) born at Norton and christened at Gainford, County Durham, England. Married Eleanor Foster (1769-1826) of Amherst, N.S. in 1790. They cleared land and established a home just south of the family homestead at the corner of Little River and Colpitts Settlement roads. There were two children: *MARGARET* b 1791 who married Benjamin Wheaton of Sackville on 5 July 1810 and *ROBERT JOHN* b 1794 who married Mary (Polly) Goodwin of Baie Verte. John died a young man of 26 and was buried in the family plot near the homestead. His widow married John Fawcet of Sackville.

ROBERT (1769-1855) born at Selaby and christened at Gainford, married Rachel Steeves of Hillsborough (descendant of Christian) and settled on Dickie Mountain near Bloomfield Station. Robert became a Baptist lay preacher and was ordained a Free Baptist minister in 1833. There were 13 children: *MARGARET* (1798-1880) m 1812 George Jonah (c1785-1871), 5 sons, 6 daus; *ROBERT* d age 7; *SUSANNA* no data; *ROSANNA* d 1889, m John Morrison d 1846, 2 sons, 2 daus; *MARY* m 1824 Rev. Edward Weyman d 1882, 6 sons, 3 daus; *ELEANOR (NELLIE)* (1809-87) m Thomas Hayes b 1801, 4 sons, 3 daus; *ANN* b 1810 m John Pierce b 1810, 4 sons, 7 daus; *RACHEL* d age 14; *JOHN WESLEY* (1813-72) m (1) 1837 Ann Pierce, 3 sons, 3 daus, m (2) Joannah S. Baxter, 2 sons, 1 dau; *JANE* (1807-85) m 1829 1st cousin Lazarus Colpitts-son of William, 5 sons; *ELIZABETH*(1818-1907) m George Sherwood (1816-86), 7 sons, 5 daus; *WILLIAM HENRY* (1820-67) unmarried; *ABRAM S.*(1823-1905) m Charlotte H. Hayes, 1 dau.

ELIZABETH b 1772 at Burtree House in Durham County, m Lewis Smith, son of James Smith from Londonderry, Ireland. Children: *ROBERT*(1794-1878) m 1818 Lavinia Babcock (1791-1884), 7 sons, 1 dau; *MARGARET* m . . . Price, issue unknown; *JANE* d c1833 m 1814 Benjamin Reynolds Jonah son of John Jonah, Hillsborough,

3 sons, 2 daus; *ANN* (1797-1869) m 1815 Isaac Steeves (1792-1887), descendant of John, 5 sons, 4 daus; *MARY* (1802-36) m 1821 Joel Steeves (1798-1871), descendant of John, 4 sons, 1 dau; *ELIZABETH* no data.

THOMAS (1773-1849) b at Burtree House in Durham, m Eunice Reynolds (1776-1861) of Lubec, Maine, settled on the Pollett River between the farms of his brother Ralph to the north and William to the south. Children: *LYDIA* b 1799 m 1813 Henry Jonah b 1793, had 1 dau; *ROBERT* (1801-96) m 1826 Mary Beck (1807-59), 10 sons, 4 daus; *ELIZABETH* (1804-71) m 1832 Michael Gowland b 1807, issue unknown; *JOHN NEWTON* (1805-46) m Margaret Kay, issue unknown; *SARAH* b 1807 m 1827 Charles Blakney b 1804, issue unknown; *NATHANIEL* (1809-52), unmarried; *WILLIAM* b 1811 m 1832 Elizabeth Stiles (1813-82), 6 sons, 5 daus; *MARGARET* (1817-80) m 1834 George Killam, 4 sons, 4 daus; *BENJAMIN REYNOLDS* (1818-86) m 1838 Catherine Bleakney (1822-93), 5 sons, 7 daus; *JONATHAN THOMAS* (1820-94) m Margaret Smith (1826-61), 5 sons, 2 daus; settled on the original homestead while the other sons established homes elsewhere on the Pollett River.

WILLIAM b 1775 at Burtree House and christened at Haugton Le Skerne in Durham County; m Elizabeth (Cummings) Stiles of Coverdale and settled on the Pollett River. Children: *ELIZABETH* (1800-85) m 1824 Isaac Turner (1794-1883) of Harvey, 5 sons, 4 daus; *CHRISTIAN* (1802-62) m 1825 Olive Weldon (1808-81) 6 sons, 3 daus (see Weldon, p. 8, 1953); *LAZARUS* (1804-70) m 1829 Jane Colpitts (1807-85) daughter of Robert and Rachel Steeves Colpitts, 5 sons; *JOHN* (1807-86) m (1) 1830 Seraphina Fillmore, 6 sons, 8 daus, m (2) Ann Grant, no children; *MARGARET* (1808-40) unmarried, buried in Middle Coverdale; *MARY* (1810-53) m 1829 Rufus Fillmore (1806-98), 3 sons, 3 daus; *LEWIS* (1813-52) m 1840 Catherine Steeves (1818-91), descendant of John, 2 sons, 1 dau; *ELEANOR* no data; *DELILAH* m 1835 Abner Jones, issue unknown.

RALPH (2, see below)

GEORGE (1782-1858) b at Kenton near Newcastle-upon-Tyne, thrice married: (1) 1806 Elizabeth Foster of Amherst b 1786 (2nd cousin), sister of John's wife, m (2) Grace Mollins of Coverdale, m (3) Elizabeth Mollins of Coverdale. George inherited his father's farm (Appendix A). He and his three wives are buried in the family plot on the intervale near the old home. There were seven children all by the first wife: WILLIAM (1807?-51), lame, unmarried; JOHN no data; ELEANOR (EMMA) b 1810 m 1831 Godfrey Mollins (1803?- 75), 4 sons, 4 daus; MARY no data; MARGARET m Thomas Nixon, no further data; CHRISTIANA (1823-1903) m (1) 1848 Charles Goodwin (1821-66) of Baie Verte, 3 sons, 3 daus, m (2) 1868 Isaac Colpitts (1818-99), a grandson of George's brother John, no issue; GEORGE b 1826 m Mary Trenholm of Pointe de Bute, issue unknown.

MARGARET (1784-1871) born at family home in Colpitts, the first Canadian born, m 1814 Jacob Day (1773-1858) of Wickham, Queen's County, N.B. Children: JACOB b 1817 m (1) Charlotte Colwell, 1 son, 2 daus, m (2) Martha Abigail Smith, no issue; GEORGE(1819-1902) m 1868 Mary Atkins Colpitts (1842-1926), grandaughter of his Uncle Thomas, 4 sons, 2 daus; ROBERT m . . . Colwell, no other data; ELEANOR (1822-82) m John Van Wart (1817-85), 5 sons, 2 daus; JOHN m Susan . . . 5 sons, 1 dau.

JANE b 1786 at the family home in Colpitts, m 1807 Christopher Horsman, Jr., and settled on the Pollett River just north of her brother Ralph. Children: MARY b 1809 m 1825 Jonathan Geldart, no further data; ROBERT (1811-99) m 1832 Rebecca Bleakney, 2 sons, 2 daus; MARGARET b 1812 m 1832 Thomas Geldart, no other data; JOHN b 1813, m 1840 Eunice Jonah b 1820, settled on the old homestead at The Glades, 6 sons, 5 daus; JANE b 1818 m 1841 James Bannister, no other data; LUCRETIA (1820-54) m 1852 John Wesley Jonah b 1819, 1 son, 4 daus; ANN b 1822, m 1841 Joseph Bannister, 4 sons, 4 daus; BENJAMIN (1826-62) m (1) 1845 Mary Ann Goodall d 1855 at age 31, 1 dau, m (2) Lavinia . . . (1831-1900), 1 son, 2 daus, Benjamin and his two wives are buried in the Old Elgin Cemetery; SARAH b 1827, no other data; ELIZABETH b 1831 James Collier, 2 sons, 4 daus.

RALPH COLPITTS SON OF THE PIONEER

(2) RALPH COLPITTS	M	(1) MARIA JONES
1778-1856	1806	d 1823
		(2) HANNAH RAYMOND
	1841	(3) EMMA MOLLINS

Ralph was born at Peathrow and christened at Cockfield in County Durham, England. He settled on the Pollett River and had ten children by his first wife Maria (Miriam) Jones of Moncton and one by his second wife Hannah Raymond of Hampton, Kings County; there were no children of his third marriage to Emma Mollins of Coverdale. Ralph's first two wives are buried in Salisbury Pioneer Cemetery; inscriptions read as follows: "Maria wife of Ralph Colpitts who d 11 Dec 1823 age 37 yrs 8 mons 26 days" and "Hannah wife of Ralph Colpitts 7 dau of Stant and Sarah Raymond d 11 March 1839 aged 46 years 3 mons 24 days." Ralph is probably buried in the cemetery near his old farm (now referred to as "Old Collicut Place"). Other details concerning this ancestor are given in Chapter 5.

The Family of Ralph Colpitts and Miriam Jones

HENRY b 1807 m 1830 Martha Beck, had one son before his accidental death during the clearing operations at Pleasant Vale (Chapter 5).

ROBERT (1808-96) m 1835 Sarah C. Weldon (1809-82), pioneer settlers in Pleasant Vale, buried in Pioneer Cemetery, Pleasant Vale. Raised 6 sons, 2 daus (see Chapter 5 and Weldon, pp. 15-23, 1953).

THOMAS (3 see below)

RALPH (1815-89) m (1) 1843 Sarah Jane Smith granddaughter of Elizabeth (Colpitts) and Lewis Smith, no children, m (2) 1847 Mary (Polly) Mollins (1827-1911), 5 sons, 4 daus; this Ralph, known as Ralph Jr., farmed the Pollett River homestead established by his father Ralph b 1778.

CHARLES d after 1900 m (1) Ann MacAnespy b 1825, 4 sons, 3 daus, m (2) Mary Charlotte Colpitts b 1838 granddaughter of William and Elizabeth (Stiles) Colpitts, no children. Daughter Olive (sixth child) married Ezra Hoar. See Chapter 5.

CHRISTIANNA m 1834 Charles McFee. 2 sons.

MARGARET JANE m 1837 Robert Jonah b 1813, son of Margaret and George Jonah, grandson of Robert and Rachel (Steeves) Colpitts, 2 sons, 4 daus.

LYDIA (1818-88) m 1838 William Perry, issue unknown.

MARIA (1823-1914) m Daniel Perry, issue unknown.

DEBORAH b 1823? m (1) 1842 Michael Thorne, issue unknown, m (2) J. Herschel Smith b 1835, grandson of Elizabeth (Colpitts) and Lewis Smith.

The Family of Ralph Colpitts and Hannah Raymond

SARAH JANE m 1847 Charles Keith, 3 sons 1 dau.

THOMAS COLPITTS OF THE THIRD GENERATION

(3) THOMAS COLPITTS	M	ANN MARGARET WELDON
1810-80	1838	1819-1901

Thomas, known to his many nieces and nephews as "Uncle Tommy," was one of the pioneers of Pleasant Vale, arriving there with his brothers to clear land and build homesteads in 1831-32. In 1838, he married Ann Margaret Weldon of Coverdale whose old home is depicted on page 90. Ann Margaret's eldest sister Sarah had married Robert an older brother of Thomas three years previously. The two brothers raised their large families in fine old homes directly across the roads from each other.

Within 19 years of their marriage, Thomas and Ann Margaret had ten children. Eight of them survived the hazards of infancy and childhood, married and raised large families of their own. The old home, shown on page 116, must have been a lively place with all the activities of a farming family and a new child arriving about every two years. Elderly relatives tell me that the third storey of the home was finished as a play area for the children. The Thomas Colpitts home was also a center of community activity since the post office (closed in 1913) operated from the part of the old home shown at the extreme left of the sketch and since Thomas was also a Justice of the Peace.

THE YORKSHIRE ANCESTRY

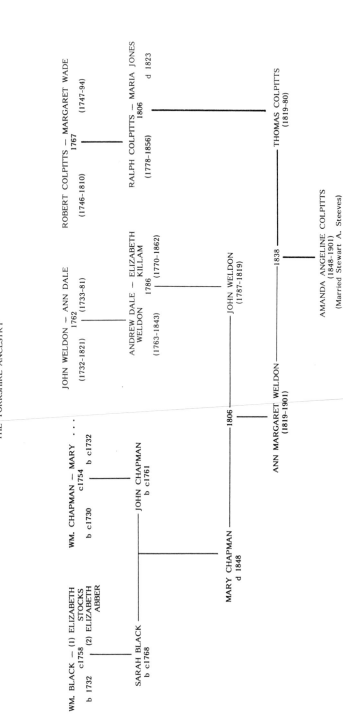

WM. BLACK — (1) ELIZABETH
STOCKS
c1758
b 1732 (2) ELIZABETH
ABBER

WM. CHAPMAN — MARY . . .
c1754
b c1730 b c1732

JOHN WELDON — ANN DALE
1762
(1732-1821) (1733-81)

ROBERT COLPITTS — MARGARET WADE
1767
(1746-1810) (1747-94)

SARAH BLACK
b c1768

JOHN CHAPMAN
b c1761

ANDREW DALE — ELIZABETH
WELDON KILLAM
1786
(1763-1843) (1770-1862)

RALPH COLPITTS — MARIA JONES
1806
(1778-1856) d 1823

MARY CHAPMAN
d 1848

JOHN WELDON
(1787-1819)

——1806——

THOMAS COLPITTS
(1819-80)

ANN MARGARET WELDON
(1819-1901)

——1838——

AMANDA ANGELINE COLPITTS
(1848-1901)
(Married Stewart A. Steeves)

Thomas lived only his allotted three score and ten years while his wife Ann Margaret lived on for two more decades. My own mother would have been 20 when her grandmother (Ann Margaret) died—the same year as her own mother (Amanda Colpitts Steeves). Among mother's mementos, we have a tin type of Ann Margaret showing a healthy lady of about 50 in a black bonnet neatly tied under her chin. There is also an unfinished sampler made by Ann Margaret, probably at age 12-13, now framed and hanging in our home.

When great grandfather Thomas died, the homestead went to his eldest son John Arthur McNutt Colpitts known as "Captain Arthur," who is said to have been a very difficult character. His wife was Abigail Charlotte Sherman known as "Aunt Abbie." They raised six children in the old home (one infant death). Arthur's two mothers (his own mother Ann Margaret and his mother-in-law Mary Sherman) were also a part of the household. They are remembered as sitting by the fire, chatting cosily, with knitting needles clicking as they turned the sheep's heavy coats into socks, mittens and woolen underwear—a necessary protection against the cold New Brunswick winters. Perhaps the two mothers were good friends; perhaps this is reflected in the fact that they share a head stone in the "new" Pleasant Vale Cemetery. Great grandfather Thomas is buried in the Old Burying Ground (Pioneer Cemetery), located on the hillside above Robert's old home in the Vale.

After Captain Arthur died in 1911, his wife "Aunt Abbie" moved to Chelmsford, Massachusetts to keep house for her unmarried children (Florence, Fred, Annie) who did office work in Boston or its suburbs. Aunt Abbie is buried in Chelmsford while her husband is interred in Pleasant Vale Cemetery; their names are on one side of the headstone that bears the names of Arthur's two mothers on the other. When I attended University in Boston (1936-39) Florence, Fred and Annie lived in Wakefield and Florence was the homemaker; this Wakefield home became one of my homes away from home.

After Captain Arthur's death, there were two more of the Colpitts relatives who lived in the old homestead—Captain George (grandson of Robert the Pleasant Vale pioneer) and Curtis Colpitts (grandson of Thomas). Old timers know the place as "The Curtis Colpitts Place." It is now owned and beautifully maintained by

131

Charles E. Barbour to whom I am indebted for a memorable tour of the house and several details mentioned here.

The Family of Thomas Colpitts and Ann Margaret Weldon

SARAH ELIZABETH (1839-1920) m 1858 Samuel W. Goggin (1832-88), of Irish descent, settled on a farm in Elgin. Children: *THOMAS ALBERT* (1859-1939) m (1) Annie Steeves, descendant of Lewis, d 1886, m (2) Araminta D. Milton (1862-1921); *CHARLES HENRY* (1861-88), unmarried. Aunt Sarah is remembered as a lady with beautiful teeth that she regularly polished with baked and crushed egg shells.

MARY JANE (1841-1931) m Ainsley B. Wallace and settled in Boundary Creek; in my childhood we visited Aunt Mary periodically; there were no children and it was a very quiet place but the wild strawberry preserves and cream of tartar biscuits were memorable.

J. ARTHUR MCNUTT (1843-1911) m 1872 Abigail C. Sherman. d 1926. They settled on the homestead of Arthur's parents as noted above. Children: *BARZILLAI A. W.* (1873-1914) m 1908 Caro Mae Cook, two children, one died in infancy; *ADA PEARL* (1877-78); *FLORENCE E.* (1881-1965), did not marry, moved to U.S. and did office work in Chelmsford where she lived with her mother and unmarried brother Fred and sister Annie, later moved to Wakefield as noted above; *FRED MIDDLETON* (1886-194-) worked in office of Colpitts Tourist Company, Boston; *STEPHEN S.* (1890-1954) m 1927 Minnie L. Avery a nurse, 2 sons, 2 daus ; Stephen also emigrated to New England and latterly lived in New Hampshire; *ANNIE EULA* (1892-1966), did office work in and around Boston. *GUTHERIE S.* (1894-1917) killed in Battle of Paschendale, World War I.

HENRY TRUEMAN (1846-1917) m 1881 Esther J. Osborne (Aunt Essie) and had eight children but six died young; *HARRY* (1888-1946), the fourth child m 1913 Pearl McKinney of Woodstock, N.B., lived in Boston area; *JENNIE* (1895-1954) the eighth child m 1918 Albert Farwell and had one child Lloyd; this family also lived in the Boston area. Aunt Essie is remembered as a lively individual; when warned by her daughter that the customs officer would not permit her to take a small plant across the Canada/U.S. border, she said "watch me" and as she approached the customs check point, she popped the plant under her hat and carried it safely to her Boston destination.

AMANDA ANGELINE (4, see below)

CELIA CATHERINE (1850-51)

STEPHEN BAMFORD WELDON (1852-1925) named for his uncle S.B.Weldon who owned the Weldon homestead in Coverdale (see p. 90), m Jane Almira Steeves (1858-1919), daughter of Ephraim Steeves—hence, the children of Amanda and Stewart Steeves were "double" cousins of those of Stephen and Jane Colpitts. At the time of his marriage, Stephen Colpitts was a carriage maker in Salisbury but later he moved to Boston where he established a successful woodworking and carriage shop in Allston; a sample of Stephen's early woodworking survives as a corner display stand in the living room of the Steeves homestead, Salisbury Road. Children: *EVA* no record, probably died young; *CLARENCE CLYDE* (1871-1964) m 1904 Matilda Osborne, no children. C. Clyde and his brother Stewart founded the COLPITTS TOUR-IST CO., located at 262 Washington St., Boston—offering "Tours of the Better Grade." An item in a Boston newspaper (1954) refers to Clarence C. Colpitts as "dean" of travel agents in New England; *HENRY TRUEMAN* (1873-94), did not marry;   *ABBIE* d 1892; *ABEL JONES* (1880-1943) m 1901 Eva Barrows, 1 dau, 2 sons; Abel was a plumber in the Boston suburb of Belmont; *STEWART ALONZO* (1883-1943) m 1903 Edith Hopkins, 1 dau and 1 son, Stewart was the prime mover in the tourist company, said to have been a more practical man than his brother Clyde. *BARBARA* (1884-87); *MARY AGNES* (1885-1972) m (1) Fred G. Barrows d 1932, brother of Eva the wife of Abel, 2 sons Fred b 1912 and Bernard b 1917; m (2) 1958 George W. Hoar (1885-1983).

THOMAS ALBERT (1854-99) m (1) Etta Armstrong who had one son *GARNET F.* before her early death; m (2) Jane Armstrong 1863-1933), four children of this marriage: *DALTON* m   Elizabeth McCully; *CURTIS* m Mary Lane, 3 daus; *ETTA* m (1) Roy Parkin, 3 daus, m (2) J.W.Kierstead, no issue; *FLETCHER* m Grace Sherwood. The Thomas Albert family farmed a property immediately south of the original Thomas Colpitts farm in Pleasant Vale; in the next generation, Dalton inherited his father's farm while Curtis farmed the original Thomas Colpitts property.

ALMIRY ANN (1857-1936) m 1880 Howard D. Stevens (1856-1928) one time farmer in Goshen and Justice of Peace for Albert County, later a pharmacist who owned a prosperous drug store in Woodstock, N.B. ("STEVENS THE DRUGGIST"); Aunt Annie was one of mother's favorite relatives, said to have been like her sister, my grandmother Amanda. Children: *ARTHUR H.* (1882-1926) m Susan Pitts, 1 son, Arthur worked for the Colpitts Tourist Company in Boston; *HARRY T.* b 1883 m (1) Grace Scott d 1941, 2 sons, 1 dau, m (2) Grace Foster d 1958 m (3) 1959 Ruby Ellsworth; Harry worked in the Woodstock drug store; *DOUGLAS W.C.* (1884-1960) m (1) Kate Dunbar d 1923, 4 sons, 1 dau, m (2) 1933 Clara Edna Dunbar. Douglas was also a druggist in Woodstock; *EDWARD* (1887-89); *JOHN CHESLEY* (1890-1967) m (1) Meda Hoyt d 1955, m (2) 1956 Idella Kinney, no issue either marriage. Chesley was a druggist in Houlton, Maine a short distance across the border from Woodstock. *MARY* b 1900 but died at birth. Aunt Annie, whom some of the cousins called "Black-eyed Annie" was killed by a "hit and run" driver when out to church on a Sunday evening.

LOUISE M. a twin sister of Almiry Ann survived only eight months.

(4) AMANDA ANGELINE COLPITTS 1848-1901	M 1870	STEWART ALONZO STEEVES 1837-1918

Amanda and Stewart were married in Pleasant Vale on New Year's Eve 1870. The only record of the happy event is the marriage certificate which survives among the Steeves Family Papers. It reads:

> This is to certify all whom it may con-
> cern, that Stewart A. Steeves &
> Amanda A. Colpitts were legally & duly mar-
> ried in the presence of witnesses, on the 31st
> of December, 1870, by me.
> Tho[s] Allen
> Wesleyan Minister

Considering the size of the family and the numbers of relatives living nearby, there were probably many witnesses and one can

Stewart A. Steeves b 1837 and Amanda A. (Colpitts) Steeves b 1848 with their family (left to right): Thomas Albert Colpitts, John Wesley and Nina Bernice.

imagine the old house throbbing with special New Year happiness. Presumably, my grandmother's honeymoon was a trip to the Steeves homestead in Boundary Creek. Glimpses of Amanda's married life are recorded in Chapter 3, while her many descendants are listed in Appendix C.

REFERENCES

Colpitts, C.D. 1967. The Colpitts from Yorkshire. Family document, typed. Not Published. (Excellent source of data for family groups but few copies exist.)

Colpitts, G.A. 1963. Pioneers of New Brunswick. The "John Branch" of the Colpitts family (1783-1963). Author Publication, Carberry, Manitoba. 133 p.

Goodwin, E.C. 1981. Robert and Margaret Colpitts. Pioneers of New Brunswick. *In* Colpitts Bicentennial Papers (1983). File in Provincial Archives, Fredericton, N.B.

Kanner, K. and Geldart, V. 1984. Marriage register 1846-1887, Albert County, N.B. Mimeographed (ISBN 0-9691642-0-3). 186 p.

Kanner, K. and Geldart, V. 1986. Marriage register Westmorland County NB 1790-1856 Part I. Mimeographed (ISBN 0-9691642-1-1). 293 p.

Weldon, W.S. 1953. The family of Weldon in Canada 1732-1952. Author Publication, Amherst, N.S. 126 p. [Since both Robert and Thomas Colpitts (third generation) married into the Weldon family, this book is an important source of several families that I have listed.]

Wright, E.C. 1965. The Steeves descendants. Author Publication, Wolfville, N.S. 923 p.

NOTES

NOTES TO CHAPTER 1

1. Prior to European settlements in the 1700s, the Micmacs numbering about 3,500, occupied Nova Scotia and Eastern New Brunswick; their neighbors to the west of the St. John River valley were the Maliseets numbering about 800; the Maliseets were the Amerindians of the St. John River valley and its tributaries in New Brunswick and Maine (Historical Atlas of Canada, Vol. 1, 1987).

2. To the Acadians, the Annapolis River was Rivière au Dauphin and the Bay of Fundy was Baie Française.

3. In my memory, our ancestors referred to a sluice gate as a "bito" (pronounced "buy-toe").

4. In 1968, a causeway was built across the river about two miles west of Moncton and changed forever the nature of the Petitcodiac estuary. West of the causeway, the waters now form a peaceful lake while downstream at Moncton extensive silting has altered the shoreline so that it is difficult to visualize Moncton as an active port with sailing ships loading lumber or unloading cargoes of molasses and other shipments from faraway places. Once an active ship building center, the bustling wharves of Moncton are now gone (Larracey, 1985).

5. A privateer was an armed private ship commissioned to cruise against the commerce or warships of an enemy; the term also applied to the Commander or one of the crew; the "prize" was a wartime capture of a ship or its cargo.

NOTES TO CHAPTER 2

1. The texts of the two Proclamations and certain other documents of this period are given in the Appendices to Raymond (1911).

2. For an account of the social and political conditions in Philadelphia at the end of the eighteenth century, see *A view of the United States of America* by Tench Coxe, Chapter 4, 1794.

3. These were not the first Pennsylvania German families to settle on the lands north of the Chignecto and Shepody Bays. Twenty German families from Philadelphia arrived in Hopewell Township in early October 1765. These settlers seem to have established themselves rapidly and formed a prosperous and thriving community (Germantown) which within two years was able to export cheese, potatoes, spruce and grindstones.

4. In Vancouver, Canada (1988) the samphire is sold at specialty food counters as "sea asparagus." It appears in salads in some restaurants on the west coast. Only the tender growing tips are marketed in 100 g plastic bags at prices that would astonish the residents of Moncton or Hillsborough. This plant is also called "saltwort." There are several varieties. A bundle of upright plants is shown in the sketch (p. 46); in one variety, the plants spread horizontally to form a plate-like mass; my mother preferred these.

5. Hence STEVESTON, the town on Lulu Island, British Columbia, named after William Herbert Steves, son of Manoah Steves, the pioneer settler from New Brunswick who moved west in 1877; Manoah was a first cousin of my grandfather Stewart Alonzo Steeves (Wright, 1961, 1965).

NOTES TO CHAPTER 3

1. "Bottom" was an old English term applied to low lying grassland along a watercourse.

2. In 1855, The Bend was incorporated as the town of Moncton, named in memory of Lt. Col. Robt. Monckton. Evidently a recording clerk at the New Brunswick Legislature dropped the "k" in transcribing the act of incorporation. Moncton was reincorporated in 1875 and its status changed to a city in 1890.

3. Dad purchased his first automobile the year sister Edith was born (1922).

4. This Family Bible, published in 1875 by the National Publishing Co., Philadelphia, is cared for by Audrey (Gaskin) Steeves, widow of Stewart A. Steeves (sixth generation). Heinrich and Rachel brought a German Bible with them to Nova Scotia in 1766; this Family Bible, printed in 1700, is in the Provincial Archives of New Brunswick. Our Stief progenitors also brought a wall clock of German origin, hand-crafted with wooden works; this dates from the early 1700s and is in the Albert County Museum. Other family treasures that survive include several pieces of fine porcelain or china from the homeland (*Moncton Daily Times,* 23 July 1966).

5. I refer to pictures of two couples that hang on the east wall of the parlor in the Steeves homestead. Family members do not know to whom these photographs belong. My guess is based on a strong resemblance of one of the ladies to Ann Margaret Weldon whose picture is in my possession. I assume that her partner is Thomas Colpitts and that these are the parents of Amanda Colpitts. It seems logical that the other couple is Ephraim Steeves and Jane Mitton, parents of Stewart Steeves. Large portraits of Stewart and Amanda hang on the south wall of the parlor.

6. Attached to this document is a 10-cm diameter seal of the Province of New Brunswick, made of bee's wax. The grant is in possession of Burton A. Steeves, grandson of Andrew G. Steeves.

7. Addresses: W.B.Oulton, P.O. Box 65, Christina Lake, B.C., Canada, VOH 1E0. Wayne Johnston, 252 Arthur Street, Oshawa, Ontario. L1H 1N6.

8. Address: 52 Scadding Street, Taunton, MA 02780, U.S.A.

9. In 1875, Andrew G. Steeves purchased the Abraham Trites farm from Frank Oulton and his wife Christiana who was the daughter of Alfred Trites. Deeds and papers in possession of Burton Steeves indicate that this property was held continuously by members of the Trites family from the time of the original land grant (1790) until purchased by Andrew Steeves. Andrew's maternal grandmother was Catherine Trites, Abraham's daughter.

10. The *Moncton Daily Times* noted Uncle John's passing in part, thus: "He was recognized as one of the best practical agriculturists and a leading dairy farmer in the Moncton district. . . . For more than sixty years Mr. Steeves . . . actively followed the career of his choice . . . . which had been that of his father and grandfather before him. . . . he strove successfully to encourage practices which would make for better agriculture. . . . For many years he occupied the position of parish clerk for the Moncton area and was also prominent in other aspects of life in the community."

11. The wedding gown was handmade by Nina's cousin Addie Charters.

NOTE TO CHAPTER 4

1. According to Cyrus Black (1855), a descendant of William Black, the pioneer William made his first voyage to Nova Scotia in May 1774; after purchasing an estate in Amherst, he returned to England in the autumn of 1774. However, ship lists for the main groups of Nova Scotia immigrants in 1774 do not include his name; perhaps he came singly or with a smaller group. Although one would expect Black (1885) to have the correct date, Milner (1934) says that William made his first voyage on the *Duke of York* in 1772. I have not researched the matter further.

NOTES TO CHAPTER 5

1. The Coverdale River is now known as the Little River and so named on current topographic maps; it appears as the Coverdale on the 1862 maps in the Public Archives of Canada.

2. . . . that mixture of fact and fancy orally communicated across the generations . . . (Taylor and Crandall, p. 10, 1986).

3. Regular mail service with Britain was not established until 1840 when Samuel Cunard initiated trans-Atlantic steam service and Halifax became the center for the distribution of colonial mails. Although pre-paid postage was introduced in Britain in 1840, this did not apply to the colonies where rates were high and the receiver, not the sender, paid the costs. Robert Colpitts had been dead for more than a quarter of a century before a weekly stage coach passed through Salisbury linking this part of New Brunswick with the Halifax post office (Campbell, 1948; Ross, 1986).

4. This was the eighth Albert County reunion of the descendants of Robert Colpitts and Margaret Wade. Places and dates of earlier gatherings were: Little River, 6 September 1900; Forest Glen, 27 August 1902; Forest Glen, 24 August 1905; Little River, 25 August 1910; Forest Glen, 2 September 1915; Little River, 26 August 1920; and Little River 25 August 1928. There have also been Colpitts Reunions elsewhere; an item from a New England newspaper dated 4 November 1961 reads: "COLPITTS ANNUAL REUNION was attended by nearly 2,400 guests last week at the Hotel Bradford.

It was the 36th annual event sponsored by the Colpitts of New England. It also marked the recent union of Colpitts, Kimball Travel Center and Carlson Travel Service."

5. Martha Colpitts b 1736 married John Atkinson and Margaret her sister, married George Forster (later Foster). The Atkinsons with their four sons and two daughters and the Forsters with their four daughters arrived in Halifax aboard the *Arethusa* in 1774. They settled on farming land at Fort Lawrence. Martha and Margaret were daughters of Thomas Colpitts (1689-1759) and Eleanor Allen and granddaughters of Thomas Colpitts and Mary Barnes who were married 14 November 1688; these Colpitts families lived in the vicinity of Barnard Castle, Durham County (Research of Sterling Marsh in Colpitts Bicentennial Papers, 1983).

6. A "yeoman" before the Agricultural Revolution, was a small-time farmer in contrast to the aristocrats who owned large estates; a yeoman owned his strips of land in various fields. A "free peasant" by contrast, contracted with his lord for the right to work a farm in return for "dues and services." A fixed amount of the peasant's produce and a definite number of days of labor per year must be given to the lord. At still another level, "serfs" were rooted to the soil, belonged to the estate and could neither leave the land nor be evicted from it. If the estate was sold, the serf, like the buildings and cattle, went with it (Schapiro and Morris, 1938).

7. The name of C. Trites appears on the Westmorland map of 1862 in the National Map Coll., Public Archives Canada (No. 13801-2/8). The names of W. Colpitts and R. Colpitts also appear in the same general area indicating that, in the nineteenth century, some members of the Colpitts family took up land near Robert's first selection. The name S.B.Weldon (another Yorkshire descendant) is also found in this area; in the 1830s, two of Robert's grandsons married sisters of S.B.Weldon.

8. At this time there were no roads worthy of the name in the Moncton area. When New Brunswick was given separate colonial status in 1784, there were still only two roads in Nova Scotia (between Halifax and Windsor and betweeen Halifax and Truro) and these were impassable for horse and wagon during the muddy periods of spring and autumn. It was mid-1800s before there was much in the way of roads in the Maritimes; during the 1820s roads were opened but still hazardous between Saint John and Moncton/Fredericton. A stage coach service between Saint John and The Bend (Moncton) was introduced in 1836; rate of passage 3d per mile with custom-

ary baggage 25s to The Bend, 30s to Dorchester and 37s 6d to Amherst. Records indicate that the journeys were often hazardous and that travel by ship was preferred. The road into The Bend from Saint John was called the King's Highway (map of 1829) but later referred to as the Cumberland Road and then the Westmorland Road or the Road to Westmorland (map of 1873). See Campbell (1948), Pincombe (1969) and Larracey (1970).

9. The long dreamed of destination of the Colpitts family was the Petitcodiac River Valley, at that time (1783) located in Cumberland County, Nova Scotia. In 1784, Loyalist demands led to the partition of Nova Scotia and the lands north of the Bay of Fundy became the colony of New Brunswick. The part of Cumberland County north of the Missiguash River in the Isthmus of Chignecto formed Westmorland County, New Brunswick. Albert, the lands south of the Petitcodiac River, did not become a separate county until 1846. Partitioning of old Nova Scotia commenced in 1869 when the Island of Saint John (Île St-Jean before 1763) formed a separate colony; its name was changed to Prince Edward Island in 1799. Cape Breton Island (Île Royale in Acadian days) was made a separate colonial jurisdiction in 1784 but this lasted only 36 years when Cape Breton was returned to Nova Scotia.

10. James Charters eventually settled north of the Petitcodiac and received land grants in Allison (near to and east of the present Baptist Church). His grant totalled 700 acres while his son Timothy acquired 260 acres [Grant Index Plans (Sheet No. 119), N.B. Crown Lands Branch, Dep't Natur. Resources and Energy].

11. The burial plot (enclosed by a corral-type fence) is evident just to the right of the bridge shown on p. 106. Jean Colpitts Waddy believes that the following are buried there: Margaret d 1794, her eldest son John d 1794, Robert the progenitor d 1810, George's three wives and his lame son William and several others (letter dated 11 February 1987).

12. In 1785, Parr Town on the East side of Saint John Harbor and Carleton on the West side were incorporated under the name of Saint John, the first incorporated city in what is now Canada.

13. Christopher Horsman and Robert Colpitts sailed together on the *Jenny* in 1775. These two young men (27 and 28 years of age) must have become well acquainted on the long trans-Atlantic voyage. Ten years later, Robert had settled on the Little River while Christopher acquired a land grant of 725 acres near The Bend (location near present Uplands School and Steeves Memorial Church). Christopher Horsman, Jr., who settled on the

Pollett River was the eldest son; his grant of 630 acres was just north of the Ralph Colpitts holdings. Four generations of Horsmans lived on this property (Christopher Jr., John, William and Horatio). The house built in 1828 is believed to be the oldest in the parish of Salisbury (Colpitts Bicentennial Papers, 1983).

Today, the Ralph Colpitts farm is referred to as "The Old Collicut Place;" it is located between Forest Glen and the Glades. The Thomas and William Colpitts holdings were directly south of Ralph's farm; thus, four of the children of Robert Colpitts and Margaret Wade settled along the Pollett River with Jane (Horsman) farthest north and William farthest south (in all about 3,000 acres of land).

14. Robert's service in the N.B. Militia may be the only basis for a family tradition that "Captain Robert Colpitts from Durham, England was sent by his Majesty's Government in 1775 to make a survey of the Bay of Fundy, including Chignecto Bay and the Petitcodiac River Valley. He was so impressed with the area that . . ." (McPhee, 1962; Colpitts 1963). However, since he is listed as a "Captain" in the Westmorland unit, he may have had some military experience as a young man.

15. I first heard of the Fenians in childhood. When my brother and I were driving mother to distraction, her worst punishment was a threat to desert us and let the Fenians get us. I realized that this would be a horrible fate but had no idea who or what the Fenians were. See Thompson (1987) for a brief account of the Aroostook (Lumberman's) War and Graves (1986) for the general activities of the Fenians.

16. I am indebted to Jean Waddy for a photocopy of this will. Suggestive evidence for Robert's marriage to Elizabeth Newton is found in the fact that Robert and Elizabeth sold the same lots of property in 1809 and that these lands had been left by John Newton to his wife (letter from Jean Waddy).

17. An act passed in 1871 provided for free non-sectarian schools and it was some time after this that rural schools became general throughout the province. An earlier act (1816) authorized a grammar school in each county; there were also some private schools in larger centers. However, it is unlikely that pioneers who carved out farms in a wilderness had either the time or the resources to take advantage of distant schools (notes based on information in the Provincial Archives, Fredericton, New Brunswick).

143

18. Maria was presumably a daughter of Charles Jones (d 1778), the founder of this branch of the Jones family in Moncton. Charles had two sons John and Henry and two daughters Margaret and Catherine. The boys were 'teen-agers when the family arrived on the Petitcodiac (1766) and since Maria's eldest was named Henry, it seems likely that her father was Henry (second son of Charles); if this assumption is correct, her mother was Christina Somers who married Henry Jones (*The Times-Transcript*, *Special Supplement* May 28, 1983). Mathias Somers (Summers) and his family were Pennsylvania Dutch arrivals of 1766. They had one son and five or six daughters (Wright, 1978). The eldest child Rachel married Frederick Stief. Thus, the Somers family was connected with both sides of my mother's ancestry (Chart p. 63).

19. Henry, the eldest of Ralph and Maria's ten children was born 15 May 1807. The records indicate that Maria died when twin daughters were born late in 1823. Ten children in 17 years was about average in healthy pioneer families, if we assume one set of twins. Two year intervals between births were common with about one year for pregnancy and one for lactation.

20. Celia Maria Colpitts (1879-1969) was the youngest of the five children of Fletcher C. Colpitts and Melissa Killam. Her grandparents were Robert Colpitts and Sarah C. Weldon and her great great-grandparents the progenitors of the New Brunswick Colpitts family. She married O.H.Bishop.

21. Although Ralph b 1815 never settled in Pleasant Vale, a petition in his name was filed for the purchase of two blocks of land (each 100 acres). The petition signed by Ralph Colpitts and approved on the payment of 20 pounds sterling on 17 February 1830 referred to two parcels of land bordering those of his brothers Robert and Thomas; these parcels were probably added to their farms (Microfilm F4212 N.B. Provincial Archives and Grant Index Plan No. 131, Crown Lands Branch, Dep't Natur. Resources and Energy, Fredericton, N.B.).

22. Henry who married Martha Beck 30 September 1830 left a son one year old when he was accidentally killed during the clearing operations of 1831-32. Henry's widow and young son James Edward Colpitts emigrated to Ohio with a group of friends; James grew up there and founded an American branch of the Colpitts family (E.C.G. in Colpitts Bicentennial Papers, 1983).

23. Built by Joe Smith 1888.

24. For the original publication see *Phil. Trans. Roy. Soc. London* 15

(171): 988, 1685. The abridged account appears on p. 156 (Vol. 3, 1809) of the same publication [Abridged Transactions from 1665-1800].

25. 40 gallons of sap are evaporated to make one gallon of syrup.

26. According to Statistics Canada, approximately two million gallons of maple syrup were being produced in Canada annually in the early 1980s (1 gal syrup = 10 lbs maple sugar). More than 85 per cent of the Canadian maple products come from Quebec and Ontario; the remaining 10 to 15 per cent from the Maritimes. The future of the industry is now threatened by acid rain (Lanken, 1987).

27. Biographical notes on many individuals are included in Chapter 6 on the Colpitts ancestry.

NOTES TO CHAPTER 6

1. Robert had one brother William, four years his senior and two sisters Elizabeth b 1728 and Dorothy b 1733.

2. The eldest son Thomas married Elizabeth Allen; two of their daughters (Martha and Margaret) settled near Fort Lawrence (see Chapter 5).

3. Notes based on correspondence with Jean Colpitts Waddy and on E.C.Goodwin in Colpitts Bicentennial Papers, 1983.

Appendix A

LAST WILL AND TESTAMENT OF ROBERT COLPITTS

In the name of God Amen. I, Robert Colpitts of Hillsborough in the County of Westmorland, being of sound mind, memory and understanding, but mindful of Mortality do make and ordain this my last Will and Testament in manner following. I commend myself, to Almighty God the giver of all mercies, and my Estate wherewith it has pleased him to bless me, I give and bequeath as follows, after my just debts are paid and Funeral Expenses and a Christian burial at the direction of my Executors, I give to my wife Elizabeth the whole of my Real Estate to hold to her during her natural life in lieu of all Dower and also my household furniture. Likewise I give to my Sons Robert, Thomas William and Ralph and to my Daughters Elizabeth Margaret and Jane and my grandchildren John and Margaret the Children of my Son John deceased the whole of my personal estate to be divided into nine equal shares and divided among them, share and share alike, but I nevertheless order and direct that the Livestock be not taken from the Farm at present but be continued on the same for the purpose of increase and improvement until the end of two years after my decease when the three first named Sons shall be intitled to their Shares, and the three next named, to receive their shares the year after and my daughter Jane and two grandchildren to receive their shares the year following. Likewise I give and devise to my youngest son George the remainder of my Real estate to hold to him from and after the decease of my wife and his heirs forever and also the remainder of the Stock on the Farm after the respective shares are distributed. Lastly, I do nominate, constitute and appoint my sons Robert and Thomas to be my executors of this my last will and Testament, hereby revoking all other and former wills and

146

pronouncing this to be my last Will and Testament. In Witness whereof I have hereto set my hand and seal the eighth day of April in the year of our Lord one thousand, eight hundred and nine.

Signed, sealed, published pronounced and declared by the Testator as his last Will and Testament, in the presence of us who subscribe our names as Witnesses thereto in presence of the Testator.

Robert Colpitts (SEAL)

A. Botsford

John Fawcet

Timothy Richardson

[A photocopy of this will is included in the paper by E.C.Goodwin, Colpitts Bicentennial Papers (1983)].

LAST WILL AND TESTAMENT OF EPHRAIM STEVES

This is the last will and testament of me Ephraim Steves of Moncton in the County of Westmorland, and Province of New Brunswick, Farmer.

I give and bequeath unto my beloved wife Jane Steves in addition to her right of dower, a suitable driving horse and carriage and harness, and farm things with sufficient hay and pasture from year to year to keep them during her life.

Also I give devise and bequeath to my son Ralph Steves all the land below the fence between me, the said Ephraim Steves and said Ralph Steves.

Also I give devise and bequeath to my daughter Naomi Wilson the sum of two hundred and fifty dollars lawful money of Canada said money to be paid the first of any legacy after my death.

Also I give devise and bequeath to my daughter Catherine Jones the sum of two hundred and fifty dollars said sum to be paid within six months from the date of my decease.

Also I give devise and bequeath to the children of my daughter Rosanna Steves wife of Jordan Steves (to wit) Edgar Milner Steves and Charles Seymour Steves and Emma Gertrude Steves the sum of eighty five dollars each said money to be paid at the several times that each of them arrives at the age of twenty one years and I further will that in the event that either of them dies before they attain the above mentioned age then the survivors or survivor will be paid the share which would have gone to the one so dying and in the further event that neither of them the said children shall live until they attain the above mentioned age of twenty one years then the said money two hundred and fifty dollars shall be equally divided between the rest of my daughters or their heirs.

Also I give devise and bequeath to my daughter Adeline Charters the sum of five hundred dollars said money to be paid a year from the date of my decease.

Also I give devise and bequeath to my daughter Barbara Steves the sum of five hundred and fifty dollars the said money to be paid within two years from the date of my decease.

Also I give devise and bequeath to my daughter Almira Jane Colpitts the sum of two hundred and fifty dollars to be paid within two years and six months from the date of my decease.

Also I give devise and bequeath to my son Andrew Steves the sum of two dollars said money to be paid in five years from the date of my decease.

Also I further order and direct the pecuniary legacies aforesaid to be paid the respective legatees by my executors hereinafter named in the order and times before mentioned.

Also I give and bequeath to my son Wesley Steves a home (to wit) which be provided with sufficient food and clothing and his room at the homestead with bed and bedding and medical attendance (?) if such should be required.

Also I order and direct that so long as my daughter Barbara Steves remains unmarried she shall be provided with house and lodging at the homestead by my son Stewart Steves.

Also I order and direct that the pecuniary legacies herein before mentioned shall be chargeable upon my real estate if my personal estate proves insufficient for this payment.

Also I order my Executors to pay all my debts after which I give devise and bequeath to my son Stewart Steves all the rest and residue (not previously disposed of) both real and personal of whatever nature or kind wheresoever situated or being (?) and hereby making and appointing him residency legatee.

And lastly I hereby nominate and appoint my sons Ralph Steves and Stewart Steves Executors of this my last will and testament hereby revoking all other wills made by me at any time heretofore.

In witness whereof I the said Ephraim Steves have hereunto set my hand and seal this thirty first day of March in the year of our Lord one thousand eight hundred and eighty two.

Signed, sealed . . . witnesses Moses Jones, Thomas L. Nixon.

[Ephraim, like many of his generation, was illiterate and made "his mark" on legal documents.]

Appendix C

DESCENDANTS OF
STEWART A. STEEVES AND AMANDA A. COLPITTS

In the lists that follow, the number sequences recording dates are day/month/year. Thus, 31.8.13 means 31 August 1913.

The John Wesley Branch

JOHN WESLEY STEEVES b 4.12.71 d 11.3.53 [Farmer] m 02.12.95 Celia Maria Wortman b 04.06.69 d 21.2.48. Daughter of Harding Wortman and Jane Mitton Ayles.

WELDON CRUSE b 18.8.97 d 15.9.81 [Shopkeeper in Salisbury] m 16.1.25 Vera E. Gillis b 18.5.00 d 3.2.56. Daughter of John Gillis and Blanche Graves.

 Herbert Gillis b 6.5.27

INFANT SON d 1.4.99

LILLIAN GERTRUDE b 18.10.00 d 4.2.77

ALBERTA AMANDA b 21.5.02 m 26.6.31 John Patrick Dunn b 23.2.95 d 11.11.46 [Salesman, Boston and suburbs]

 Joan Patricia b 10.4.32 [Registered Nurse] m 2.7.55 L.W.Cronkite, Jr., M.D. b 4.5.19. Divorced.

 Judith Brown b 13.4.57 [B.A. (Maine), Marketing]
 Marcia Joan b 4.11.58
 Janice Steeves b 6.7.60 [Performing Arts - Dance and Entertainment]
 Wendy Sands b 8.6.63

John Steeves b 6.6.33 [B.Sc. (Amherst), Resort owner and operator, Rockport, Mass.] m 7.10.62 Leigh Henderson b 19.9.38 [B.A. (Amherst)].

John Steeves b 25.6.68
Robert Blackman b 19.3.73

Elizabeth Anne b 22.10.37

STEWART ALONZO b 18.3.04 d 30.4.64 [Merchant, Riverview, N.B.] m 26.2.26 Audrey Edith Gaskin b 29.4.03 [Teacher]. Daughter of John Gaskin and Eunice Jane Bennett.

John Stewart b 14.11.26 [Airline pilot] m 2.7.49 Helen Loggie b 27.3.25.

Ronald John b 3.8.52 [Airline pilot] m 6.12.80 Helen N. Burke
    Lauren Grace b 7.4.87
Jean Elizabeth b 12.9.54 m 19.9.81 Timothy Geoghegan [Dentist]
    Sean Thomas b 13.12.84
    Tera Helena b 13.12.84
    Julian Dana b 21.6.87

Paul Stewart b 8.4.56 [Airline pilot] m 28.7.86 Alyson Jane Moffatt.

Catherine Ruth b 13.7.31 [Registered nurse] m 3.5.54 Stanley C. Wood [Shopkeeper, Highways foreman] b 4.11.27 d 28.3.78. Son of David N. Wood and Ethel Gillis.

Jane Ruth b 24.6.55 [Accountant]
Joyce Elizabeth b 21.9.56 [Safety systems technician, airforce reserves].
David Stewart b 30.9.57 [Cook] m 17.5.80 Darlene L. Macdonald   b 26.12.60
Daughter of Clayton Macdonald and Myrna Cole.

    Jennifer Catherine b 25.9.80
    Christine Margaret b 16.1.83
    Dennis Andrew David b 7.2.86

Margaret Ann b 18.11.58 d 18.11.58

Kelly Joan b 1.1.61 m 26.6.82 William P.H.Barkus b 28.9.57.

LOUIS EPHRAIM b 22.1.06 d 27.9.63 [Farmer, Highways Dep't] m 22.1.42 Etta Cochrane b 22.2.16

Marylin Joyce b 20.2.43 Died at birth.
Margaret Ann b 19.10.45 d 30.5.47
Phyllis Louise b 4.10.48 m 19.4.75 Brian Lutes [Insurance agent].
    Angela Dawn b 6.10.75
    Jeffrey Brian b 26.9.79

Steeves and Colpitts Pioneers

The Nina Bernice Branch

NINA BERNICE STEEVES b 4.1.81 d 24.1.57 m 3.9.12 George Whitfield Hoar b 25.1.85 d 3.12.83 [Farmer/Dairyman]. Son of William Clark Hoar and Carolyn Lavinia Newcomb.

WILLIAM STEWART b 31.8.13 [O.C., B.A. (U.N.B.), M.A. (U.W.O.), Ph.D. (Boston), F.R.S.C., D.Sc. (Hon U.N.B., Memorial, St.FX., U.W.O.), LL.D. (Hon S.F.U., Toronto), Professor, U.B.C.] m 13.8.41 Margaret Macrae Mackenzie b 18.1.09 [B.A., M.A. (U.W.O.)]. Daughter of Angus Mackenzie and Isabella Macleod.

   Stewart George b 4.7.42 [B.Sc. (U.B.C.), Marketing James River Co.] m 11.7. 64 Linda Lucille Macleod b 23.4.43. Daughter of Donald Duncan Macleod and Ruth Alice Haraldson.

      Donna Marie b 10.1.66 [B.A. (West. Wash.)]
      Erik William b 7.2.67

   David Innes b 26.12.43 [B.Sc. (U.B.C.), Ph.D. (Calif., Davis), Biochemist/ Geneticist, Univ. Calgary] m (1) 25.1.63 Gwendoline Anne Hunt b 24 6 44 [B.A. (U.B.C.), Legal Librarian]. Daughter of Roy Hunt and Josefine Florence Harling. Divorced. m (2) Noreen Lilian Rudd b 3.9.40 [M.D. (U.B.C.), Prof. Paediatrics, Univ. Calgary]. Daughter of Robert Francis Rudd and Rose Emily Jones.

      Geoffrey David b 14.8.63 [Salesman]
      Jennifer Anne b 29.8.67

   Kenzie Margaret Newcomb b 16.9.46 [B.A. (U.B.C.), Librarian] m 16.2.85 William Edward Stacey b 15.4.54 [Hospital Orderly]

   Melanie Francis b 10.1.49 [B.A. (St. Andrews)] m 9.9.71 William Robert Galloway b 9.10.47 [B.A. (Wits), M.A. (St. Andrews), Ph.D. (Queens), Business Teacher]. Son of Alexander Leslie Galloway and Charma Lockhart Rae Whyte.

      Fiona Margaret b 30.4.75
      Alexander James b 9.8.76
      Natasha Leah Jodie b 21.12.83 [Adopted]

GERALD GEORGE b 18.11.14 [Farmer/Dairyman] m (1) 1.9.37 Doris Evelyn Worden b 11.1.14 d 5.10.63 [Teacher] m (2) 4.6.65 Laura Catherine Stiles b 6.1.29 [B.A. (Acadia), B.Ed. (U.N.B.), M.R.E. (Bibl. Sem., N.Y.)]. Daughter of R. Weldon Stiles and Dorothy Smith.

Arnold Worden b 19.9.38 [Owner and Manager/White Frost Village] m 16.8.60
Nancy Lynne Robinson b 6.3.41. Daughter of Stanley Frank Robinson and
Shirley Eileen Steeves (descendant of Christian).

Deborah Joan b 15.1.62 m (1) 15.10.83 Dale Mackenzie. Divorced. m (2)
27.5.88 Arthur Lloyd Tucker b 31.10.66

Kristin Lynne b 6.6.88

Glen Gerald b 14.12.64

Carolyn Joan b 5.5.40 [Teacher] m 23.1.65 Douglas Allen Steeves b   27.10.41
Adopted. [B.Sc. (Mt.A.), B.Ed.,   M.Ed.   (U.N.B.),   Teacher/Administrator
Community College]. Son of Austin Milton Steeves (descendant of Frederick)
and Willa Delilah Johnson.

Brian Douglas b 3.12.67
Bradley Allen b 25.10.69
Wanda Doris b 19.5.71 [Adopted]

EDITH AMANDA b 13.5.22 m 4.6.52 Calvin Othit Ogilvie [Artisan] b 20.6.27
Son of Jacob Leroy Ogilvie and Bertha Viola Ogilvie.

Heather Irene b 11.8.60 [Adopted] m (1) 18.3.77 Jerry Joseph Richardson
b 25.5.61. Son of Albernie Richardson and Jean Young. Divorced.   m (2)
14.2.86 Hudson Hugh Bass b 18.10.62. Son of Melbourne Bass and Roberta
Bremner.

Jeffrey Alan (Richardson) Saunders b 15.4.80
Justin Neil Bass b 20.8.85

Holly Jean b 24.6.62. Adopted. [Registered Nurse] m 24.6.86 Peter Murray
Jones b 10.7.64 [Bank Manager]. Son of George Stephen Jones and Charlotte
Flemming

Debbie Lee Hrechka Ogilvie b 5.3.82

Steeves and Colpitts Pioneers

The Thomas Albert Colpitts Branch

T. ALBERT C. STEEVES b 23.3.84 d 23.2.40 [Postal Clerk] m 7.2.05 Minnie Earl Hoar b 20.3.83 d 27.7.66. Daughter of William Clark Hoar and Caroline Lavinia Newcomb.

LAURNA AMANDA b 17.9.05 d 21.10.87 [B.Sc. (Mt.A.), Teacher/Home Economics, Moncton, N.B.]

STIRLING STEWART b 24.6.07 d 21.11.64 [Plumbing/Electrical Work] m (1) 1932 Lena McHaffey d 1944 m (2) 30.11.45 Ruth Elizabeth White.

Myrna Sharon b 3.3.40 [Registered Nurse] m Bill Shields [N.S. Tech, Engineer] Divorced.

Pamela
Paul
Jill
Danny

Howard Thompson b 27.12.48

CARRIE BELLE b 16.9.08 [B.Sc. (Mt.A.)] m 27.12.35 William Havelock MacKenzie b 19.9.10 d 2.4.74 [B.A. (Mt.A.), Ph.D. (Columbia), Superintendent Schools, Saint John, N.B.]. Son of John Edward MacKenzie and Sarah Jardine.

Judith Isabel b 1.10.40 [M.A. (Edinburgh)] m 16.10.71 Robert Andrew Leon [M.A. (Oxon), Chartered Accountant] b 9.9.41. Son of Peter Leon and Phyllis Isaacson.

Marcus Serge b 2.10.73

Lorna Jean b 8.5.42 [B.A. (McGill), LL.B. (U.N.B.), Lawyer/N.B. Gov.] m 14.4.62 David A. Prebble [B.Sc. (McGill)]. Son of Paul Prebble and Eva Steadman. Divorced.

Anthony David b 24.3.68
Robin John 3.1.71
Amy Carolyn b 23.5.73

Roderick William b 2.11.43 [Q.C., B.A. (Dal.), LL.B. (U.N.B.), Lawyer] m 30.9.67 Françoise Mathieu b 16.2.46 [M.A. (Amiens), Teacher]. Daughter of Jean Mathieu and Ghislaine Flabert.

Ghislaine Margarette b 15.10.77
Camille Monique b 28.12.80

WILLIAM HORACE b 11.9.09 d 1965 [B.Sc. (Mt.A.), Ph.D. (McGill), Chemist]
m 1932 Doris Calkin Cole b 20.6.13 [B.A. (Mt.A.)]. Daughter of R. Warren
Cole and Ethel Hickey.

Lowell Calkin b 6.4.33 [Salesman] m (1) 23.6.56 Thetis Wyndlow. Daughter
of George Wyndlow and Margaret Helen Rowan. Divorced. m (2) 1974 Barbara Kellett.

Christopher Philip b 29.8.57 m 2.4.88 Susan Elizabeth Bennett
Melanie Catherine b 17.3.60 m 3.12.83 Paul William Percey

Nicolle Jessica b 30.8.86

Julia Margaret b 21.8.61

Richard Allison b 2.2.38 [M.D. (U.W.O.), Ph.D. (Toronto), Radiation,
Oncologist] m 17.7.65 Eliane Brunet b 29.9.40. Daughter of Gaston A.
Brunet and Simonne A. Magé

Pascal William b 14.9.66
Colin Richard b 31.1.71
Rachel Simonne b 2.4.74

"The naming of children
is culturally
never a trivial act."

Daniel Scott Smith. Quoted p. 216 in
GENERATIONS AND CHANGE (1986).

ALLISON EARL b 1.11.10 [B.Sc. (Mt.A.), M.Sc. (McGill), D.Eng.(Tech. Univ. N.S.), Past-Pres. T.U.N.S.] m 14.1.39 Audrey Florence Arthur b 21.12.14. Daughter of Orville James Arthur and Annie Lavina Sutton.

Allison Audrey b 17.12.39 [B.Sc. (Mt.St.V.), Dietician] m (1) 9.12.58 John Andrew Miner b 27.4.37 [B.Ed. LL.B. (Dal.)]. Divorced. m (2) 11.10.80 Henricus Burgers b 24.6.27 [Ph.D. Engineer/Architect, LL.B., M.Hosp.Admin. (U.Ottawa), Chief/Hosp.Admin. Providence Villa]. Son of Henricus Burgers and Sophia Wilhelmina Van Der Hijden.

Kathryn Audrey Miner b 6.6.59 [B.A. (Mt.A.)] m 28.3.80 Richard Dubreuil [B.A. (Mt.A.)].

    Sarah Audrey b 31.1.81
    Colin James 3.3.84
    Sylvia Claire b 12.11.85
            29.12.
    Laura Andrea Miner b 12.11.67

Daryl Joyce b 3.6.42 [B.A. (Mt.A.), B.Ed. (Dal.), B.Mus.Ed. (Toronto), Music Teacher] m 4.11.67 William Chaddock b 7.1.40 [B.A. (St.Mary's), B.Ed. (Dal.), Teacher]. Son of W.A.Chaddock and Lillian Asby.

    Monica Joyce b 4.6.70
    Kirsten Sarah Allison b 13.2.72
    Charmaine Foye b 3.11.77 74
    Paul William Steeves b 11.3.77

Phyllis Lorraine b 29.12.43 [Banking Services] m 8.9.67 Richard Wayne Fullerton b 5.4.46 [B.Sc. (Dal.), M.Ed. (Toronto), Human Resources Manager]. Son of Bentley D. Fullerton and Bessie M. Akerley.

    Charles Andrew b 13.5.69
    Tamara Lee b 21.2.71
    David Edward b 24.9.74
    Erica Jane b 18.5.79
    Amanda Gail b 16.3.80

David Albert b 4.10.46 [B.Com. (St.Mary's), Chartered Accountant] m 15.2.68 Pamella Young b 4.8.47 [B.Ed. (Dal.)]. Daughter of Captain John Young and Rosemary Woodward.

    Geoffrey Mark b 23.2.73
    David Matthew b 22.11.74

THOMAS ALBERT COLPITTS b 13.3.12 [B.Eng. (N.S.Tech.U.), Food Business] m 19.11.38 Marjorie Charlotte McFarlane. Daughter of Frank E. McFarlane and Violet McClure Hammond.

Dennis McFarlane b 26.8.40 [B.Com. (U.B.C.), Business] m 17.5.63 Sheila Leslie Allin b 23.9.42. Daughter of Melville Luke Allin and Bernice Ruth Biggs.

Thomas Allin b 27.9.65
Christopher Allin b 30.6.69

Joyce Marilyn b 25.1.42 [B.Ed. (U.B.C.), Teacher] m 27.7.63 William Wilfred Lissimore b 7.8.38 [B.Sc. (U.B.C.), Teacher]. Son of Alfred James Lissimore and Marguerite Emma Dulcie.

Timothy James b 6.2.70
Darren Sean b 26.9.71

Wendy Carolyn b 25.1.42 [B.Ed. (U.B.C.), Teacher] m 22.12.62 George Barry Morgan b 29.9.41 [B.Sc. Agr. (U.B.C.), Chief Food Inspection/Health Protection]. Son of William Stephen Morgan and Bertha Ormerod.

Carolyn Elizabeth b 26.4.68
Michael Bruce b 31.12.69
Steven George b 12.4.71

1820-1950 The proportion of biblical names remained roughly constant, and the whirl of fashion caused nonbiblical favorites to rotate like the colors of a kaleideoscope— ever changing and yet always the same. . . . That . . . tendency also appeared in another aspect of the modern American naming system— in the fantastic ingenuity parents used to express a spirit of individuality in the names they gave their children.
From D.H.Fischer in GENERATIONS AND CHANGE (R.M.Taylor, Jr. and R.S.Crandall, Eds.) 1986

INDEX OF FAMILY NAMES

Surnames of all relatives are listed but, with a few exceptions, given names are only added for the Colpitts and Steeves families and for the direct descendants of Stewart A. Steeves and Amanda Colpitts Steeves. Bracketed numbers following the names indicate generations. Thus, Heinrich is first generation Steeves (1.0) while Robert is first generation Colpitts (0.1). The author of this book is (6.6), a sixth generation descendant of Heinrich Stief and Robert Colpitts.

162

GENERAL INDEX